AMACHE REMEMBERED

AMACHE:
An American Concentration Camp
1942-1945

Robert Y. Fuchigami

Copyright 2020 by Robert Y. Fuchigami.

Published 2020.

Printed in the United States of America.

All rights reserved.

No portion of this book may be reproduced, stored in a retrieval system, or transmitted in any form or by any means – electronic, mechanical, photocopy, recording, scanning, or other – except for brief quotations in critical reviews or articles, without the prior written permission of the author.

ISBN 978-1-950647-62-0

Publisher's Cataloging-in-Publication data

Names: Fuchigami, Robert Y., author.
Title: Amache remembered : Amache : an American concentration camp 1942-1945. / by Robert Y. Fuchigami.
Description: Parker [Colorado] : BookCrafters, 2020. Paperback.
Identifiers: ISBN: 978-1-950647-62-0
Subjects: LCSH: Granada Relocation Center. | Japanese Americans. | World War, 1939-1945—Concentration camps—Colorado—Amache.
BISAC: HISTORY / United States / 20th Century.
Classification: LCC D769.8.A6 | DDC 940.531778 FUCHIGAMI–dc22

Publishing assistance by BookCrafters, Parker, Colorado.
www.bookcrafters.net

Table of Contents

Amache Remembered..1
Dedication...3
Acknowledgements..5
Special Thanks..7
Amache Guard Towers...10
Terminology...12
Civilian Exclusion Order No. 5...14
Introduction..17
Prologue..19
Significant Quotations...24
Bill of Rights Violated..29
Population Fact Sheet..32
Fact Sheet: Granada Relocation Center.............................34
    Amache Ochinee Prowers..38
    Granada Relocation Project — Amache, Colorado..............40
    Community Description..41
    Inmate Housing...42
    CommunalFacilities...43
    Basic Services...44
    Educational Program...46
    Community Governance...47
    Recreation and Leisure Time..47
    Employment in Amache...48
    Amache Farm Agricultural Operation...............................49
    The People of Amache — Displaced Americans................49
    Military Service...50
    Resisters of Conscience..52
    100th Infantry Battalion and
        442nd Regimental Combat Team..................................53

    NISEI Military Intelligence Service Unit
       During World War II..54
    Relocation and Resettlement..58
    Statement of Facts (All Centers Meeting in 1945)....................61
    Registration and Re-segregation...63
    Life in Amache..65
    A Typical Day in Amache...67
    Some Questions Needing Answers...70
    Positives and Negatives of the Amache Experience................71
    Resident Inmates Stories..73
    Some Final Comments...86
    Summary — Who, What, Where, When and Why.................88
    Governor Ralph Carr...91
    List of Persons Who Died in Amache...93
Two Amache Mysteries..95
Remembering Amache: Past, Present and Future.......................98
Pilgrims and Reunions..102
On Executive Orders: Then and Now..103
A Key Question Answered...107
    Colonel Karl Bendetsen
    The Man Who Put Us into the Camps......................................108
Appendices...115
An Apology from the California State Grange..............................116
Comprehensive Interpretive Plan..117
    Site Background..118
    Statements of Significance..118
    Primary Interpretive Themes and Subthemes....................119
Senate Bill 2870, Introduced May 16, 2018......................................123
Presentation Romero Theatre Group...127
About the Author..130
Bibliography...132

"There are times when history fails to record certain vital facts either because of neglect or shame – and the story is lost in the shadow of greater events, until it becomes nothing more than a legend."

"During World War II, over one hundred thousand American citizens were corralled behind barbed wire with watch towers, search beacons and armed guards, simply because they had Japanese faces and names. These people have earned a place in history; they have earned the right to have their story told. No myth or legend this: Amache's pain and suffering were real and true."

Alice M. Coleman,
Lest We Forget. Pg. 112.
Cummings and Hathaway Publishers. 1992.

Dedication

THIS BOOK IS RESPECTFULLY DEDICATED to the Issei generation, to Heita and Tokuye Fuchigami, my parents, and all other Issei immigrants from Japan who came to the United States for a variety of reasons and survived despite continual efforts to deny them full equality and participation in American society. They faced enormous political, legislative, social, and economic obstacles.

Politically they had to cope with racist attitudes held by leaders of a variety of civic, social, fraternal, political, labor and military organizations. On the West Coast, the attitudes were directed toward all Asians and people of color in general.

They had to deal with legislative acts that denied them American citizenship and ownership of land. Laws were passed to prevent intermarriage with persons from other racial groups. In 1924 a law was passed which virtually stopped further immigration of persons from Japan to the United States.

Socially they were excluded from membership in all organizations listed earlier. They were not allowed to use community facilities such as swimming pools, golf courses, etc. In some communities their children had to attend separate schools. They were even buried in separate areas of cemeteries.

They had difficulty getting loans and were restricted in employment opportunities. Even their children could not obtain jobs in areas where they had been educated and trained. University and college graduates in engineering, law, teacher training, etc., were unable to find employment and had to settle for jobs as gardeners, produce market clerks, or waiters in ethnic restaurants.

The Issei generation survived it all with pride, patience, perseverance, and dignity. They had one over-riding thought: a better life in America for their children. They worked long hours and made incredible sacrifices to provide the basic necessities and education they believed were required to succeed in America.

Their successful struggle for survival in a hostile environment will remain as a lasting source of inspiration for us who had the privilege of having them as our parents and grandparents.

Acknowledgements

IN 1999, PORTIONS OF THIS PUBLICATION were written for a grant awarded me by the California Civil Liberties Public Education Program (CCLPEP) to develop activities and educational materials that ensure for future generations' remembrance of the forced removal and incarceration of U.S. citizens of Japanese ancestry and Japanese alien residents during World War II. The CCLPEP program was created through legislation known as the California Civil Liberties Public Education Act, or AB 1915 (Chapter 570 Statues of 1998). The legislation was introduced in the California State Assembly in 1998 by Mike Honda of San Jose. Honda later went on to become a respected member of Congress for many years. As a very young child Honda lived in Amache.

In 2018, friends encouraged me to update and revise the publication since new information had become available. Since moving to Evergreen, Colorado, in 2005, I joined the Amache Club, Friends of Amache, Mile High chapter of JACL, Japanese American Association of Colorado, and continued association with Minoru Tonai and the Amache Historical Society based in Los Angeles, California. A treasured friendship was developed with John Hopper of Granada, Colorado, who provided amazing leadership, wisdom, and vision for the many preservation and restoration activities at Amache over the past 30 years.

The following list of names is but a tiny portion of those who assisted me since my return to Colorado: Jim, Kerry and Calvin Hada, Kara Miyagishima, Derek Okubo, John Hopper,

Bill Convery, Min Tonai, Frank Miyazawa, Hiroko Hung, Vicki and Marge Taniwaki, Dan Yoshii, Doug Shinsato, Bonnie Clark, Lawson Inada, Jane Daniels, Roy Hatamiya, Mary Masunaga, Chiyo Horiuchi, James Walsh, Sues Hess, Tracy Coppola, and many, many others.

I am particularly indebted to my wife Sally, for her great assistance on all phases of the project. She spent countless hours organizing materials and providing continual support for the project. Thank you also to my daughters Kathleen Marie and Ellen Suzanne for their continual interest, encouragement, and assistance.

Robert Fuchigami
Evergreen, Colorado. 2020

Special Thanks

PEOPLE WHO KNOW THE HISTORY of the Amache site, visited the Amache Museum in Granada, or associated with former residents at Amache are aware of the countless contributions of John Hopper and his past and present students in their preservation and restoration activities. John Hopper is a unique individual. He has dedicated his life to preserving and restoring the Amache site and its history. When he began teaching at Granada High School in 1993, he learned that the abandoned and deteriorating Amache site was a perfect opportunity to help his students learn this part of American history through a "backyard hands-on" experience. He was supported in his novel visionary educational approach by his school superintendent: Ian DeBono. John Hopper and his students were successful beyond their wildest dreams. His students learned to conduct research, learned to make oral presentations to a wide variety of audiences, write original papers, and even produce a monthly newsletter for widespread distribution.

Not only did they educate themselves and the residents of Granada and neighboring towns, but they were invited to make presentations about Amache to schools, colleges, and public in Colorado, Kansas, Oklahoma, and even Japan! The trips to Japan were made available through the sponsorship of the Japanese Consul General's office in Denver, whose representative visited the Amache site during annual pilgrimages. Throughout the years, former residents of Amache have expressed their profound thanks to Mr. Hopper and his students. As a person who has watched his students make presentations on several occasions in the Denver area, I would like to humbly add mine. He is, indeed, a rare and remarkable individual.

Another individual who deserve special recognition is Minoru (Min) Tonai of the Amache Historical Society based in Los Angeles. As an Amache teenager, Min had a keen interest in history and moved freely around the camp, making observations that others did not. Min was a natural leader, recognized as such by all who became acquainted with him. His detailed remembrance of sights seen, events occurred, and people involved, have helped historians, anthropologists, and former Amacheans immensely over the years. Min's association with Amache reunions began in 1977 when he and George Saiki co-chaired a 1978 reunion in Los Angeles. For more than 30 years, Min and his associates at the Amache Historical Society (AHS) planned reunions, provided leadership, and funded many activities to support John Hopper and the Amache Preservation Society. On one occasion AHS gave over $30,000 to help the neighboring town of Holly when it was devastated by a tornado. When funds were needed to build a memorial to Governor Ralph Carr on Kenosha Pass in Colorado, Min asked several of his friends to assist and about $15,000 was provided. When I am asked a question about Amache for which I have no answer or have doubts, I contact Min who provides the necessary information.

Amache Watch Tower 1944
https://Amache.org/photo-gallery

AMACHE: An American Concentration Camp 1942-1945

**Concentration camp:
a camp where persons are detained or confined."**
Source: *Webster's Ninth New Collegiate Dictionary*

Amache Guard Towers

THERE WERE EIGHT GUARD TOWERS strategically placed around the perimeter at Amache. Each was manned day and night by armed military policemen with rifles pointed in toward the inmates. Search lights at night probed the barracks and occasionally followed the inmates as they made their way to the latrine/laundry building.

Guard towers and barbed wire fences were the two most powerful images of the loss of freedom experienced by the over 7,500 Japanese American inmates of Amache during World War II. If the statue of liberty symbolizes freedom, the guard towers and barbed wire fences would be the very opposite of the symbol of freedom. A guard tower can be the focal point for any discussion of the entire evacuation and incarceration experience for visitors to Amache. Questions can be posed: who, what, where, when, how, and why. What about constitutional questions related to habeas corpus, hearings, and justice for all? Why did Amache have guard towers?

The young guards who manned the structures were minimally trained with orders to shoot if necessary. An interview with a woman inmate who had an encounter with a guard in a tower is revealing and troubling:

Guard: "Hey you."
Inmate: "You want to talk to me?"
Guard: "Yeah. Are you a human being?"
Inmate: "Yes. Don't you think so?"

Guard: "Yeah. You look like a human being, but where I came from in South Carolina, they said that a Jap is not a human being. They are like a gorilla so if you want to, kill them. That is what I learned when I came. And then I looked from top every day and you people look like a human being and you people all wear beautiful clothes."

Inmate: "Because old clothes, we throw that away and then select one suitcase, good clothes only, so…"

DENSHO interview series.
Copyright 1997. Inmate: Mutsu Homma

Terminology

THIS PUBLICATION WAS ORIGINALLY titled *Amache: A Concentration Camp in Colorado* because it was "a prison camp in which political dissidents, members of minority ethnic groups, etc., are confined" (*Webster's New World Dictionary – 2nd Concise Edition*). The term was used without much controversy by Presidents, politicians, the media, and others during the incarceration of Japanese Americans. There is a long history of the term. For example, it was used to confine the Cherokees and other Native Americans in the 1830s. It was used by the U.S. again in the 1899 during the Philippine-American War. In the 20th Century, the term was used by the Nazis along with the term "extermination camp."

A **concentration camp** is not necessarily a death camp. Pierre Moulin wrote the book *American Samurais: From USA Concentration Camps to the Nazi Death Camps in Europe.* Moulin explains that the camps in Germany should have been called death camps or extermination camps for places like Auschwitz, Triblinka, etc. The term "concentration camp" is now commonly used by Japanese American to describe the camps in which they were incarcerated. I have used it extensively in the text of this publication without apology to those who have on occasion objected to the use of the term, or when I have spoken publicly about incarceration in Amache. I chose not to use it as a title this time, because "Amache Remembered" is more accurate for this publication, even though we did live in a concentration camp.

Other terms used in this publication are less controversial but should be addressed. Some people have objected to the terms "evacuation" and "evacuees." **"Evacuation"** refers to temporary removal with implications that those affected could return as quickly as possible. **"Evacuee"** refers to persons who choose voluntarily to move away from danger and move back when they feel inclined to do so. In the case of Japanese Americans, the proper terms should have been **"eviction"** and **"inmates,"** or **"incarcerees"** because removal from their homes, farms and businesses was not voluntary nor justified, and they were certainly unable to return as soon as possible. "Inmates" and "incarcerees" are more accurate terminology, because we were placed in prison type facilities, complete with barbed wire enclosures, unhealthy housing, surrounded by guard towers manned by armed military policemen, and we were forced to live communally without freedom.

I use the terms **"evacuee," "Evacuation," "evacuated," "relocation," "assembly center," "relocation center,"** and sometimes **"resident,"** as those terms were used in the Granada Pioneer camp newspaper when I was in Amache. Those terms are still in use, as noted in my memories of camp. As I have learned, the term "internee" should not be used because we were not in internment camps run by the Justice Department. For more information about euphemistic terminology and how it was used during our incarceration, consult the work of Professors Roger Daniels, Gary Okahiro, and others, including DENSHO and Wikipedia.

One term used by the government during the eviction process was "non-alien" instead of "citizen." We were citizens by virtue of having been born in the United States. The term does not appear in any dictionary, as it was invented to confuse the general public.

Two of every three evacuees in Amache were American citizens, as they had been born in the United States. They were the **Nisei** (second generation) or **Sansei** (third generation). A sub-group of Nisei was the **Kibei**, persons born in the United States who had been sent by their parents to Japan for education in the language and culture of Japan. Almost a third of the evacuees in Amache were **Issei**, or immigrants from Japan.

Civilian Exclusion Order No. 5
Western Defense Command and 4th Army
Wartime Civil Control Administration
Presidio of San Francisco, California
April 1, 1942

INSTRUCTIONS
TO ALL PERSONS OF
JAPANESE
ANCESTRY
LIVING IN THE FOLLOWING AREA:

ALL THAT PORTION OF THE CITY and County of San Francisco, State of California, lying generally west of the north-south line established by Junipero Serra Boulevard, Worchester Avenue, and 19th Avenue, and lying generally north of the east-west line established by California Street, to the intersection of Market Street, and thence on Market Street to San Francisco Bay.

All Japanese persons, both alien and non-alien, will be evacuated from the above designated area by 12:00 o'clock noon, Tuesday, April 7, 1942.

No Japanese person will be permitted to enter or leave the above described area after 8:00 a.m., Thursday, April 2, 1942, without obtaining special permission from the Provost Marshal at the Civil Control Station located at:

1701 Van Ness Avenue
San Francisco, California

The Civil Control Station is equipped to assist the Japanese population affected by this evacuation in the following ways:

1. Give advice and instructions on the evacuation.
2. Provide services with respect to the management, leasing, sale, storage or other disposition of most kinds of property including: real estate, business and professional equipment, buildings, household goods, boats, automobiles, livestock, etc.
3. Provide temporary residence elsewhere for all Japanese in family groups.
4. Transport persons and a limited amount of clothing and equipment to their new residence, as specified below.

THE FOLLOWING INSTRUCTIONS MUST BE OBSERVED:

1. A responsible member of each family, preferably the head of the family, or the person in whose name most of the property is held, and each individual living alone, will report to the Civil Control Station to receive further instructions. This must be done between 8:00 a.m. and 5:00 p.m., Thursday, April 2, 1942, or between 8:00 a.m. and 5:00 p.m., Friday, April 3, 1942.
2. Evacuees must carry with them on departure for the Reception Center, the following property:

    a. Bedding and linens (no mattress) for each member of the family;
    b. Toilet articles for each member of the family;
    c. Extra clothing for each member of the family;
    d. Sufficient knives, forks, spoons, plates, bowls and cups for each member of the family;
    e. Essential personal effects for each member of the family.

All items carried will be securely packaged, tied and plainly marked with the name of the owner and numbered in accordance with instructions received at the Civil Control Station.

The size and number of packages is limited to that which can be carried by the individual or family group.

No contraband items as described in Paragraph 6, Public Proclamation No. 3, Headquarters Western Defense Command and 4th Army, dated March 24, 1942, will be carried.

3. The United States Government through its agencies will provide for the storage at the sole risk of the owner of the more substantial household items, such as iceboxes, washing machines, pianos and other heavy furniture. Cooking utensils and other small items will be accepted if crated, packed and plainly marked with the name and address of the owner. Only one name and address will be used by a given family.

4. Each family and individual living alone, will be furnished transportation to the Reception Center. Private means of transportation will not be utilized. All instructions pertaining to the movement will be obtained at the Civil Control Station.

Go to the Civil Control Station at 1701 Van Ness Avenue, San Francisco, California, between 8:00 a.m. and 5:00 p.m., Thursday, April 2, 1942, or between 8:00 a.m. and 5:00 p.m., Friday, April 3, 1942, to receive further instructions.

J. L. DeWitt
Lieutenant General, U.S. Army
Commanding

Introduction

ON FEBRUARY 19, 1942, PRESIDENT FRANKLIN D. ROOSEVELT signed Executive Order 9066 authorizing the U.S. Army Western Defense Command under Lieutenant General John L. DeWitt to be able to evacuate aliens and U. S. citizens of Japanese ancestry off the West Coast to other parts of the nation. A plan for removal and incarceration of inmates was conceived by Karl Bendetsen, a member of DeWitt's staff who transferred from Washington, D.C., for this very purpose. The military established a Wartime Civilian Control Administration (WCCA) and Bendetsen was placed in charge of carrying out his plan for removal of the Japanese Americans to the initial collection points called "assembly centers."

The inmates were given short notice (usually one week) to dispose of their properties through sale or storage, if available. Most had to sell their household goods at a fraction of its value, since everyone knew the situation. They had to go to a designated place for transportation by bus or train to the "assembly centers" located in former horse racing tracks – Santa Anita and Tanforan – and county fairgrounds such as those built in Salinas, Merced, Fresno, Stockton, etc. Some inmates were housed in smelly horse stalls instead of hastily erected tar-paper covered wooden barracks. These collection compounds had the appearance of prisons, complete with armed military police units, sentry towers, searchlights, and jeep patrols around the barbed wire enclosures surrounding the housing area.

On March 18, 1942, President Roosevelt issued Executive

Order 9102, which created the War Relocation Authority (WRA), a civilian agency to replace the WCCA, to manage the inmates at the wartime relocation centers. Milton S. Eisenhower (younger brother of Dwight Eisenhower) was appointed Director. The WRA issued detailed guidelines that were used by the inmates to build "pioneer communities" in the relocation centers. On June 19, 1942, Eisenhower resigned and was replaced by Dillon S. Myer, who remained as WRA Director until the agency was ended in June, 1946.

In the assembly center/pioneer communities, the inmates organized, developed, managed and operated the following:

- Mess halls to feed the inmates.
- Camp newspaper.
- System of self-government with an elected community council which reported to the governing authorities.
- An extensive recreation program.
- Postal system for communication and commerce.
- Canteen/store for sundries and incidentals.
- Education program for children.
- Religious services for different denominational groups.
- Camp maintenance work crews.
- Staffing for essential basic services such as fire, police, and emergency medical units.

After four months in the "assembly centers" the government moved the inmates by slow moving trains to more permanent concentration camps or "relocation centers." Upon arrival in the concentration camps, the inmates were faced with the daunting and formidable task of again building "pioneer communities," except this time on unfamiliar arid, desert or swamp type lands, and in much more extreme climatic conditions, as compared to the west coast, from where they came.

Prologue

BETWEEN DECEMBER 1941 AND MARCH 1946, almost all persons of Japanese ancestry living in California, Oregon, Washington, parts of Arizona, and the territory of Alaska, were evacuated and incarcerated for varying lengths of time (several months to four years) in assembly centers, detention facilities, and/or internment camps. While the term "concentration camp" was not officially used in government documents, it was commonly used by many observers. The relocation/concentration camps were located in remote and desolate areas of Arizona, California, Colorado, Utah, Wyoming, Idaho and Arkansas.

Our government incarcerated an entire group of Americans solely because of their ethnicity, without any charges of wrongdoing or determination of their guilt or innocence. It was an un-American act completely out of character, unjustifiable, and one that would cause other nations in other times to question the moral credibility of the United States whenever our nation attempted to get them to address abuses of civil and human rights against their own citizens. Distinguished Yale Professor of Law, Eugene V. Rostow stated the case succinctly: "Our wartime treatment of Japanese aliens and citizens of Japanese descent on the West Coast (was) hasty, unnecessary, and mistaken."

In 1983, the U. S. Congressional Commission on Wartime Relocation and Internment of Civilians issued its report entitled, Personal Justice Denied. The Commission concluded after its exhaustive investigation that "military necessity," the rationale used by our government to carry out its actions was invalid. Instead, the Commission concluded that the real reasons for the exclusion, evacuation and incarceration were 1) race prejudice, 2) war hysteria, and 3) failure of political leadership.

Comprehensive, detailed documentation and discussion of the entire exclusion, evacuation, incarceration, relocation and resettlement period is available in numerous books and articles. Rather than repeat the information, this publication will focus on a single relocation/concentration camp: Granada Relocation Project, or Amache.

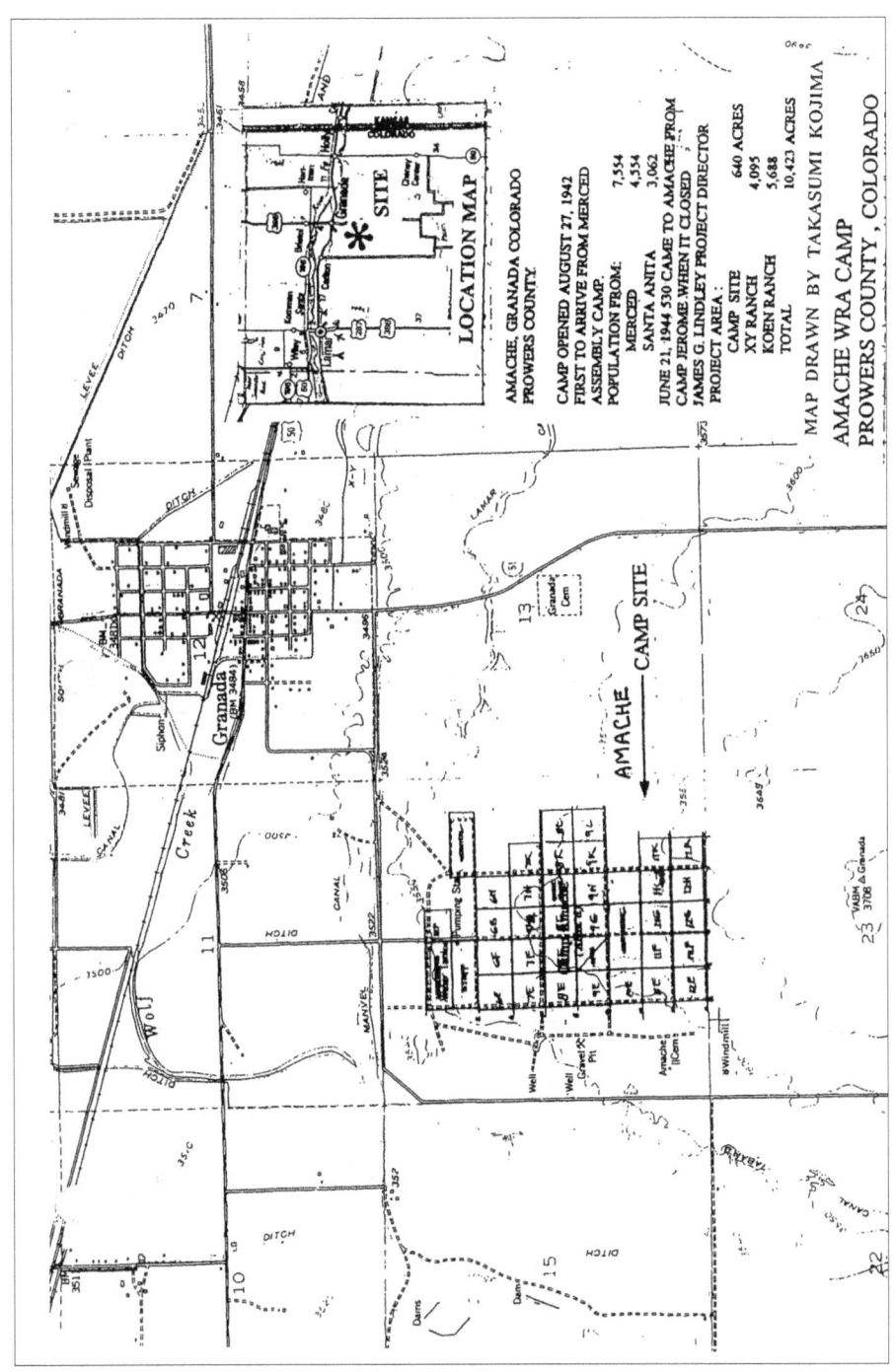

Location of the Amache Camp
https://Amache.org/photo-gallery

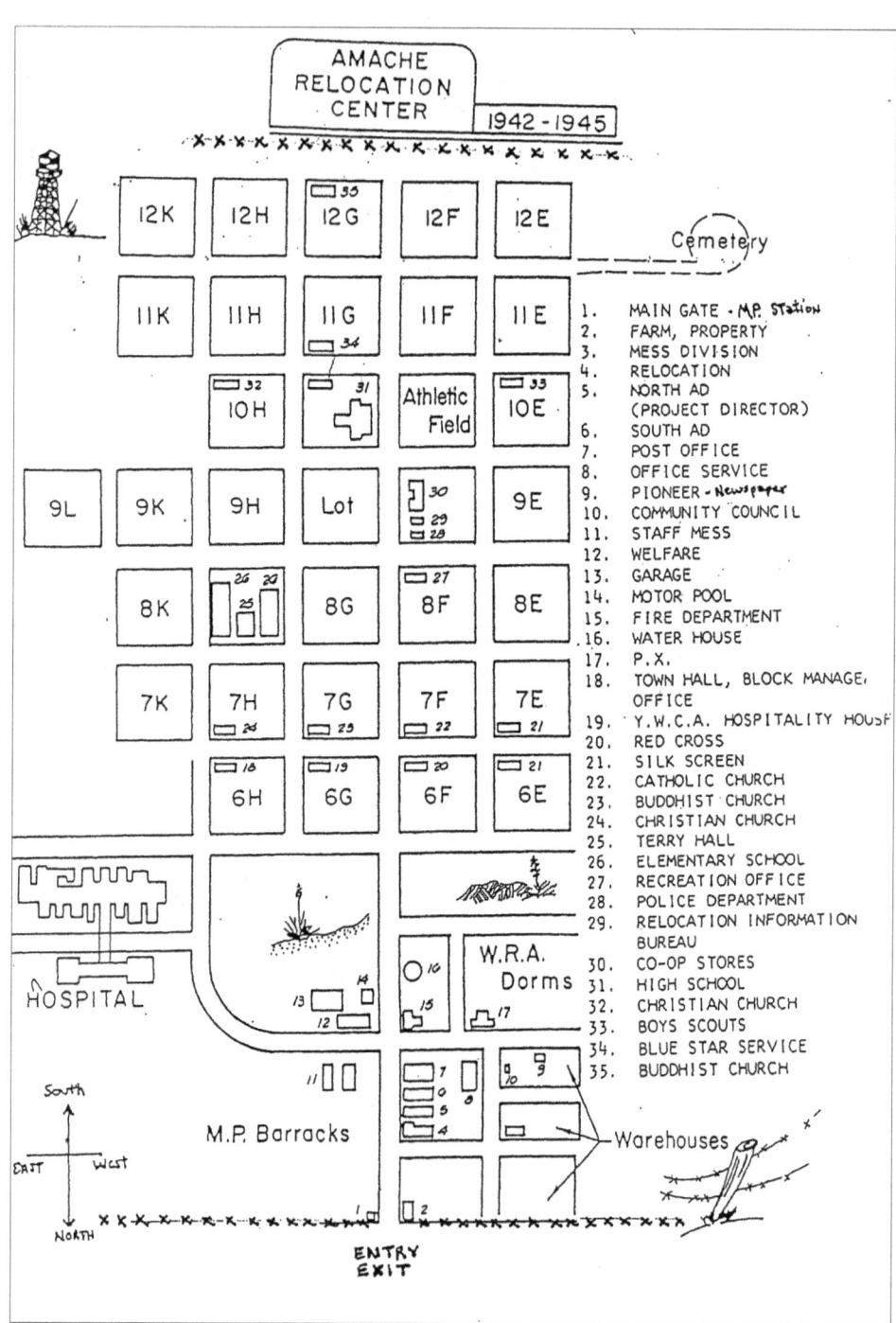

Amache Relocation Center
https://Amache.org/photo-gallery

Photograph of Amache Camp
https://Amache.org/photo-gallery

Significant Quotations

"I call upon the American people to affirm with me this American Promise – that we have learned from the tragedy of that long ago experience forever to treasure liberty and justice for each individual American, and resolve that this kind of action shall never again be repeated."

—President Gerald R. Ford
(Proclamation issued in the Bicentennial Year [1976] after remarks reviewing the removal of persons of Japanese ancestry from the West Coast during WWII.)

"We can never fully right the wrongs of the past. But we can take a clear stand for justice and recognize that serious injustices were done to Japanese Americans during World War II. In enacting a law calling for restitution and offering a sincere apology, your fellow Americans have, in a very real sense, renewed their traditional commitment to the ideals of freedom, equality and justice."

—President George Bush
(Issued in October 1990 in a statement to all living persons of Japanese ancestry directly affected by their exclusion from California and parts of Oregon Washington and Arizona.)

"This was the worst violation of constitutional rights in the history of the country. The message is, don't let it happen again."

—Governor Gary Locke
(Statement from the former governor of the state of Washington on March 31, 2007, during the 65th anniversary of the evacuation of Japanese Americans from Bainbridge Island, Washington.)

"The internment of Japanese Americans during World War II was one of the darkest moments in our nation's history – a moment when fear led us to compromise our most fundamental rights. Today, as we once again weigh the demands of security and liberty, let's remember that it's in times like these – times of great national challenge – when our ideals of justice and equality are tested most, and when it's most important that we uphold them."

—President Barack Obama
(Issued February 19, 2008, when he was a senator from Illinois.)

Concentration camp: a camp where persons (as prisoners of war, political prisoners, or refugees) are detained or confined.

—*Webster's 9th New Collegiate Dictionary*

"When a majority of the members of the Supreme Court of the United States established a precedent by validating the evacuation orders in the case of Korematsu v. United States, Justice Robert M. Jackson, in his dissenting opinion point out that the ruling 'lies about like a loaded weapon ready for the hand of any authority that can bring forward a plausible claim of an urgent need.'"

—Justice Robert Jackson

"I was surprised to learn that some of the many Island rumors about the Hawaiian Islands during the first few days of the war are still prevalent on the mainland. They have been repeatedly denied by all authorities...

"Having been in charge of military intelligence activities since June 1941, I am in a position to know what has happened. There have been no known acts of sabotage, espionage, or fifth column activities committed by the Japanese in Hawaii either on or subsequent to December 7, 1941."

—Colonel Kendall J. Fielder, G.S.C., A.C. of S.G-2
Headquarters Hawaiian Department
Office of the Assistant Chief of Staff for Military Intelligence

"I want to make an unequivocal statement in regard to the Americans of Japanese ancestry who, being American citizens, fought by our side in the war. Had it not been for the loyalty, fidelity, patriotism, and ability of these American Nisei, that part of the war in the Pacific that was dependent upon intelligence gleaned from captured document and prisoners of war would have been a far more hazardous long-drawn out affair.

"The United States of America owes a debt to these men and to their families that it can never fully repay. At a highly conservative estimate, thousands of American lives were preserved and millions of materials were saved as a result of their contribution to the war effort. It should be realized, also, that this group of men had more to lose than any other participating in the war in the Pacific."

—Colonel Sidney F. Mashbir, Commander
Allied Translator and Interpreter Services in the Pacific

General Charles Willoughby, General MacArthur's Chief of Staff for Intelligence, stated that the Nisei (who serve as Military Intelligence Service personnel) shortened the war in the Pacific by two years when they enabled the Allies to learn the real strength of the Japanese army.

The 100th Infantry Battalion and the 442nd Regimental Combat Team fought some of the most deadly battles in France and Italy against the Nazis and came out of the war as the most highly decorated unit for its size and length of service in U. S. military history. On July 15, 1946, the 442nd was honored by President Harry S Truman at a parade in Washington, DC, upon their return to the United States. Truman stated: "You fought not only the enemy, but you fought prejudice – and you have won."

Anne Reeploeg Fisher ended her book *Exile of a Race* with the following statement:

> "The Debt of Dishonor is paid. The Book is closed, the accounting inscribed on the pages of eternity:
> The Guilty – buried with their guilt
> The Greedy – to the victor belongs the spoils
> The Betrayers – paid their thirty pieces
> The Shysters – decorated with medals of honor
> The Racists – satiated
> The Military – unprecedented power
> The Constitution – a broken shield
> The Supreme Court – three dissents
> The United States – a tarnished heritage
> The People – burdened with blame and shame
> The Robbed – declared guilty
> The Innocent – condemned to the third generation
> The Future – a loaded weapon ready for The Hand

Finally, some statements from the final report of the Project Director of Granada Relocation Center (Amache), James G. Lindley, dated November 15, 1945:

> "A paragraph is necessary to express my feelings toward the evacuees. I have a lasting and deep regard for them. It is hard for one to visualize any other group of people who would be so well-behaved under similar conditions. In close contact with them over three years, I can only admire their cheerful acceptance of unfair treatment; their overcoming of fear, resentment and frustration; their willingness to give their time and effort to make various phases of the WRA program work...
>
> "They are people – even as you and I. Capable of assimilation into our western civilization, they bring to it a love of beauty, a time factor which we Westerns are in danger of ignoring, a recognition of the need of courtesy and politeness in our everyday dealings. It is my hope that through their dispersal throughout the country, both they and their neighbors will benefit by mutual association and that something good will come out of this 'piece of wartime folly'."

Bill of Rights

ALL BILL OF RIGHTS listed below were partially or totally ignored and violated when the U.S. government incarcerated the Japanese Americans during WWII:

Amendment I
Congress shall make no law respecting an establishment of religion, or prohibiting the free exercise thereof; or abridging the freedom of speech, or of the press; or the right of the people peaceably to assemble, and to petition the government for a redress of grievances.

Amendment II
A well-regulated militia being necessary to the security of a free state, the right of the people to keep and bear arms shall not be infringed.

Amendment III
No soldier shall, in time of peace be quartered in any house, without the consent of the owner, nor in time of war, but in a manner to be prescribed by law.

Amendment IV
The right of the people to be secure in their persons, houses, papers, and effects, against unreasonable searches and seizures, shall not be violated, and no warrants shall issue, but upon

probable cause, supported by oath or affirmation, and particularly describing the place to be searched, and the persons or things to be seized.

Amendment V

No person shall be held to answer for a capital, or otherwise infamous crime, unless on a presentment or indictment of a grand jury, except in cases arising in the land or naval forces, or in the militia, when in actual service in time of war or public danger; nor shall any person be subject for the same offense to be twice put in jeopardy of life or limb; nor shall be compelled in any criminal case to be a witness against himself, nor be deprived of life, liberty, or property, without due process of law; nor shall private property be taken for public use, without just compensation.

Amendment VI

In all criminal prosecutions, the accused shall enjoy the right to a speedy and public trial, by an impartial jury of the state and district wherein the crime shall have been committed, which district shall have been previously ascertained by law, and to be informed of the nature and cause of the accusation; to be confronted with the witnesses against him; to have compulsory process for obtaining witnesses in his favor, and to have the assistance of counsel for his defense.

Amendment VII

In suits at common law, where the value in controversy shall exceed twenty dollars, the right of trial by jury shall be preserved, and no fact tried by a jury, shall be otherwise reexamined in any court of the United States, than according to the rules of the common law.

Amendment VIII

Excessive bail shall not be required, nor excessive fines imposed, nor cruel and unusual punishments inflicted.

Amendment IX

The enumeration in the Constitution, of certain rights, shall not be construed to deny or disparage others retained by the people.

Amendment X

The powers not delegated to the United States by the Constitution, nor prohibited by it to the states, are reserved to the states respectively, or to the people.

Population Fact Sheet

In 1940, 126,947 persons of Japanese ancestry lived in the 48 United States. The percentage of their population in the U.S. was only one tenth of one percent. Almost 90 percent of them lived in California (93,717), Washington (14,565) and Oregon (4,713).

In the Hawaiian Islands (not yet a state) there were 158,000 persons of Japanese ancestry. They comprised 37 percent of the island's population. Pearl Harbor is located on the island of Oahu. Only 1,118 (one percent) of the Hawaiian Islanders were evacuated and incarcerated, while almost all Japanese Americans in the three western coastal states were incarcerated.

In 1941, the population of Japanese ancestry consisted of 2/3 American citizens born in the U.S., and 1/3 born in Japan. The Japan born individuals were unable to become U.S. citizens because of discriminatory legislation. It was not until 1952 that the elderly Japanese born in Japan became eligible for U.S. citizenship.

Not a single documented act of espionage, sabotage, or fifth column activity was committed by an American citizen of Japanese ancestry or by a resident Japanese alien on the West Coast or in Hawaii, despite wild rumors and lies reported by the irresponsible Hearst and McClatchy news organizations.

Colonel Karl Bendetsen ruled that all persons of Japanese ancestry (including orphans with a single drop of Japanese blood) would have to be sent to concentration camps. The orphans at the Maryknoll facility in Los Angeles were sent to the Manzanar camp.

Constitutional rights and civil liberties of Japanese Americans were simply violated and ignored. Contrary to the basic idea that a person is presumed innocent until proven guilty, the Japanese Americans were considered guilty until proven innocent. No charges were filed. Attorney General of California Earl Warren and others supported the absurd notion that the absence of any negative actions by Japanese Americans was somehow "proof" that they were capable of doing something wrong and were just waiting to do so because of their ancestry!

The military moved all Japanese Americans in California, the western half of Oregon and Washington and part of Arizona into "assembly centers" and "relocation camps" beginning in March 1942. Most of the "evacuees" were given about a week, or less, to sell, lease or find someone to care for their homes, businesses, personal property, precious possessions, family pets, etc. Each person was allowed only what he/she could carry. It was a traumatic and chaotic few days for all family members since they were not told where they were going or how long they would be gone. Millions of dollars were lost during the process.

Three types of confinement sites were used to incarcerate the persons of Japanese ancestry:

- Assembly Centers operated by the military (WCCA). Santa Ana race track, Merced, etc.
- Relocation Centers operated by the civilian War Relocation Authority (WRA). Amache was one.
- Department of Justice Internment Camps. (Included Germans and Italians at Crystal City, Texas)

A fourth type was used solely for Japanese Army and Navy military Prisoners of War captured in the Pacific war region. Most of the Japanese POWs were confined at Camp McCoy, Wisconsin.

Fact Sheet: Granada Relocation Center, Amache Concentration Camp

LOCATION: PROWERS COUNTY, Colorado. One mile west of Granada, 17 miles east of Lamar.

Project Director: James G. Lindley

Project Size: Amache 640 acres (One mile square surrounded by barbed wire fence and guard towers manned by armed military police)

Koen Ranch 5,688 acres (The Koen and XY ranches were used as farm land

XY Ranch 4,095 acres   to raise various crops and livestock.)

Total: 10,423 acres

Construction of Amache began on June 29, 1942. Over 1,000 workers were used to clear the sagebrush covered land and to build 349 military type barracks, plus large multiple-use mess halls, communal use latrines, showers and clothes washing facilities for the evacuee/residents. In total, the workers built 569 structures for the project, including various administrative buildings and warehouses, a hospital, sewage plant and pond, fire station, police station, a water system, a small post office, a military police compound, guard towers, as well as a system of roads and a perimeter of barbed wire fence to surround the camp. A cemetery and columbarium were built outside the fenced area. The construction work was still in progress when the first residents began arriving on August 27, 1942. A high school and a cooperative store were completed in 1943.

Population: October 1942 – 7,567 inmates were living in Amache. Most of the residents were from California (4,492 were from the Merced Assembly Center, and 3,092 from the Santa Anita Assembly Center). Assembly centers were civilian collection centers for persons of Japanese ancestry. Separate from the Japanese American population were about 150 Caucasians (white) Americans who served as administrative staff with the WRA (War Relocation Authority), civil servants involved in the supervision of relocation planning and assistance, employment, agriculture, engineering, community service, and administrative management. In 1942 a Military Police contingent of 134 soldiers were housed at Amache for assignment to the guard towers, to patrol the perimeter of the fence, prevent escapes and check passes for persons entering and exiting the camp. Later the number of MPs was reduced to 15.

Housing of inmates: The barracks for inmate/residents were divided into 29 blocks. Each block had 13 barracks, a mess hall, and a multipurpose H-shaped building housing separate toilet and shower facilities for men and women, and wash basins for cleaning clothes. One of the barracks in each block was designed as a recreation hall for the block residents, but in fact were used for such things as churches, Boy Scout offices, camp newspaper office, camp store (before the consumer cooperative building was built), and meeting places for a variety of clubs. The other 12 barracks in each block were used by residents for sleeping purposes. Each barrack was 120 by 20 feet, and divided into six "apartments." Each apartment housed a maximum of seven persons. While most apartments accommodated a family of five to seven people, in some instances an apartment would house a group of bachelors or two sets of small, unrelated families. The barracks were poorly insulated, a single layer of brick for the floor, had no running water, no toilet facilities, and only a single light bulb. There was no furniture except for canvas camping cots, thin cotton mattresses, and a round pot-bellied stove for burning coal. Each block housed approximately 250 residents.

Communal mess halls, toilets and showers: Residents lined up to use the toilet and showers, lined up three times daily to eat at common mess halls, and lined up to use the washbasins for laundering clothes.

The people: Two of every three residents were American citizens by birth. The other third were older Japanese who were born in Japan, but who had immigrated to the U.S. in the early 1900s. These Japanese were not allowed to become citizens due to discriminatory legislation. The residents from the Merced Assembly Center were primarily from the rural farming sections of California's central valley and the San Francisco Bay area. The residents from Santa Anita were primarily urban dwellers from the Los Angeles area. In Amache there were merchants, doctors, lawyers, scientists, jewelers, optometrists, gardeners, hotel and restaurant operators, salesmen, clerks, artists, chicken farmers, agricultural workers, fruit stand operators, architects, musicians, day laborers, students, college professors, and even one opera singer. There were rich and poor, healthy and the disabled.

With the rich diversity of talent and skills of the people, it was not surprising that the residents quickly organized themselves into a productive work force to build a vibrant "pioneering community" similar to the towns and cities they came from. They started a newspaper, staffed the hospital, manned the police and fire department, worked in the education department, served as clerks in the administration offices, organized and operated consumer cooperative enterprises, worked on the farm units, and operated the silk screen shop.

One source of discord was the pay the government provided for the work performed by the residents. The pay scale for the employees was $8 to $19 dollars per month! Professional workers like doctors and teachers earned $19; non-professionals were paid $16, and unskilled workers $8-12 per month. In contrast, the WRA workers were paid prevailing outside wages.

An active recreation program was developed by the residents to meet the varied interests of both young people and adults. Sports programs, adult education classes, youth clubs and organizations, and special events were organized and operated by the residents.

Military involvement: Amache residents were deeply interested and involved in the war going on outside the camp. They purchased war bonds and stamps, and the Boy Scouts collected tin foil. Amache young men and women served in the Armed Forces. The Amache Honor Roll included 953 names; among them, 31 who lost their lives fighting overseas. Over 100 Amache men were wounded in battle while serving in both the European and Pacific areas of conflict.

Leaving camp: Some Amache residents left camp to begin or complete interrupted college education, while others left to seek employment opportunities in Denver, Chicago, New York, etc. Some left camp temporarily to help harvest crops for farmers in Colorado, Kansas, Nebraska, etc. Others left camp to begin life anew in states like Michigan, Pennsylvania, New Jersey, Ohio. Others left camp to join the military as soldiers and nurses. Most Amache residents stayed in camp until 1945, when it was disclosed that all of the camps would be closed and residents allowed to return to the West Coast states from which they had been so unjustly evicted.

Amache Ochinee Prowers

THE GRANADA RELOCATION CENTER was named for Amache Ochinee, the beautiful daughter of warrior sub-chief Ochinee of the Southern Cheyenne Indians. Ochinee, also known as Lone Bear or One-Eye, was killed during the Sand Creek massacre of Indians by Colonel Chivington and his troops in November, 1864.

In 1861, John W. Prowers, age 23, working as a freighter of goods and supplies for Colonel Bent, met and married Amache, who was only 15 years old. The young couple purchased a small ranch and started to raise cattle.

In 1865, the government compensated each Indian who had lost a parent or been widowed by the slaughter at Sand Creek with an allotment of 160 acres. Amache and her mother each acquired some choice hay land. Prowers bought the allotments of other Indians and expanded his ranching operation. Eventually, Prowers owned almost two-thirds of the land along the Arkansas River between Lamar and Las Animas. The Prowers raised nine children: Mary, Susan, Katherine, Inez, John Jr., Frank, Leonard, Ida and Amy. Prowers became a wealthy and prosperous Coloradan before his death in 1884. In 1890 Amache married Daniel Keesee and moved to Boston. She died on February 22, 1905, and is buried in Las Animas next to John Prowers. In 1889, Bent County was split into two parts and the new county was named for Prowers.

The concentration camp was named for Amache when the

postmaster at Granada, unable to cope with the overwhelming amount of mail for inmates, requested the government build a separate post office to meet their needs. The mailing address for the Granada Relocation Project was Amache, Colorado.

Amache Ochinee Prowers
https://Amache.org/photo-gallery

Granada Relocation Project, Amache, Colorado

ONE OF THE MOST UNUSUAL COMMUNITIES in American history was Amache, tenth largest city in Colorado from late August 1942 to mid-October 1945. Today, little exists to let visitors know of its unique and significant history.

The Granada Relocation Project was located in the Arkansas River Valley, about one mile west and one-half mile south of the small town of Granada in southeastern Colorado. The entire Granada Project encompassed 10,423 acres. Amache, the barbed wire enclosed housing compound occupied by the Japanese American inmates involved 160 acres; only a small portion of the total project. The remaining 10,263 acres were used to raise and feed livestock animals, such as cattle and chickens, and to grow various types of vegetables to feed the approximately 7,500 inmates and several hundred non-inmate civilian and military personnel living and working in Amache. In fact, there were two parts to the Granada Project: one part was the Amache farm operation and the other was Amache, the inmate housing compound.

The War Relocation Authority (WRA) was the governmental agency responsible for the daily operation of the ten relocation centers. The centers were under the military umbrella of the Western Defense Command and a military police unit was assigned to each camp.

In the spring of 1942, James G. Lindley, a metallurgical

engineer by training and a former administrator with the Federal Soil Conservation Service, was selected as Project Director for Amache. Early in the construction stage of Amache, Lindley revealed his inherent fairness, compassion and sensitivity when he was able to remove the projected barbed wire fence planned to separate the administration area from the inmate housing area. Later, when housing units were built for WRA personnel, Lindley moved his family from Lamar, a nearby town, to Amache and enrolled his only daughter in school with the inmates. His trust and respect for the inmates did not go unnoticed. Because of his caring and competent leadership, Amache had the lowest number of problems during the incarceration period of the 10 concentration camps.

Lindley stated his goals and objectives for Amache as follows: 1) temporary housing and subsistence; 2) an orderly community in which to live; 3) education and training for youth and adults; and 4) relocation.

Community Description

At first glance, visitors to Amache would have noticed the similarity in appearance between the community and an Army military camp because of the rows of barracks, the barbed wire surrounding the perimeter, and the military police guard stationed at the entrance. Amache also resembled a prison because of the eight sentry towers with searchlights and jeep patrol roads around the perimeter. After entry, the differences between a military installation and a camp for civilians were quite apparent.

Upon entering Amache, the visitor would see a variety of buildings and barracks which housed administrative offices. To the left was the military police area, motor pool area, WRA staff mess hall and the Amache hospital. About one third of a mile up the main road were the inmate housing barracks clustered in blocks: 6E, 6F, 6G, 6H, etc.

Inmate Housing*

Amache consisted of 30 identical blocks of barrack type buildings. One block was set aside for the schools. Each block had 13 barracks; twelve for housing and one for recreation. In addition to the barracks, each block had two large buildings to be used by all of the block residents. One was the mess hall for meals and the other was a multiple use building with a laundry section; two sections for latrine and showers separated for men and women, and a small recreation area. A small office for the block manager was also in the multiple use building. While each block had a barrack designated for recreation, in many blocks the recreation barrack was converted for use by community wide groups and organizations such as the Red Cross, Boy Scouts, Blue Star Mothers, Nursery School, and various church denominations. Approximately 250 persons were housed in each block. In October 1942, the inmate population was 7,567 persons.

Each barrack was 120 feet long and 20 feet wide, divided into six rooms or apartments. The two largest rooms were 25 by 20 feet, the middle two were 20 by 20, and the end units were 15 by 20 feet. Each room housed four to seven persons. In several cases unrelated inmates or couples without children were forced to share the same room. Newly married couples were especially embarrassed by the lack of privacy under such conditions.

The barracks had no water; therefore, no toilets, no washbasins, and no kitchens. While every room had a small round, coal burning stove and a canvas cot for each inmate, there was no furniture: no chairs, tables and shelves. The rooms had a single layer of brick for a floor. Each inmate was issued two wool blankets.

Since Amache was still under construction, the inmates salvaged scrap wood from barrack construction sites to build crude chairs, tables, shelves and partitions for their bare rooms. The women purchased cloth from mail order catalog stores to make curtains and bed covers.

*In 1942, the War Relocation Authority considered building tent cities as relocation centers. "Had canvas for great tent cities been available, it would have been used. Tents would have been pitched and evacuees would then have gone to work building their new wartime homes. Unfortunately, canvas could not be obtained." (Source: The War Relocation Work Corp. War Relocation Authority pamphlet. 1942. Pg. 6.)

The barracks were so hastily and poorly constructed that summer wind storms blew fine sand into the rooms and winter blizzards deposited loose snow on the inside of windowsills. Thin wall partitions separated the rooms in barracks, but inmates had to monitor noise levels, conversations and disagreements to avoid disturbing occupants of neighboring rooms.

In contrast, WRA personnel who lived in Amache had residential housing units with one or two bedrooms, kitchens and bathrooms. Most of the WRA staff lived in nearby towns and commuted to their jobs in Amache. They would eat in a separate mess hall and shop in a PX store built for their use.

Communal Facilities

Because the barracks did not have water, inmates had to use communal washrooms, group showers and latrines. Women were particularly appalled and embarrassed by the inadequate partitions between toilets, the absence of doors for the toilet stalls, and minimal partitions in shower areas. There were no partitions in the men's latrine and shower area. The sick and elderly were particularly handicapped by the absence of toilets in their rooms. With winter nighttime temperatures dropping well below zero, or frequent sandstorms that obscured visibility to a few feet, the need to use communal latrines in those conditions created a major inconvenience for the less-able inmates.

The communal laundry area had concrete washtubs with scrub boards for washing clothes. The washed clothes were hung to dry on outdoor clotheslines and moved inside whenever there were dust storms, rain or snow.

Communal mess halls were 100 by 40 foot buildings with

picnic type tables arranged in orderly rows for evacuees to sit at during meals. The mess hall had refrigerators, sinks and ranges. The kitchen crew, including the cooks, were all inmates – most inexperienced in food preparation for large groups of people. Three times daily the inmates would line up for their rations. Meals in Amache were bland, but adequate. The government budget allotment for rations was 45 cents per day for each inmate. Later, when Amache farm products were harvested to augment the food supply, the food allotment was reduced to 31 cents.

Communal facilities made it difficult to maintain family unity in Amache. Some families tried to meet and eat together as a unit, but many families were unable to coordinate schedule, as their children ate with playground peers. Because assigned apartment rooms were so crowded, most family members used them only for sleeping.

Most activities were in communal facilities: eating, toileting, showering, washing clothes, recreation, etc. Parent control and monitoring of their children's activities and behavior therefore diminished rapidly. Strong family bonds were strained or broken as individual family members moved or drifted apart. Some families never recovered their pre-war family unity.

Basic Services

Churches: Religious freedom was exercised in Amache with services provided by various denominations including Catholics, Protestants, Buddhists and others. Church meetings were held in converted recreation barracks and the Block 8H mess hall.

Community Stores: The Amache Cooperative Enterprise developed and operated by inmates included a shoe department, clothing store, shoe repair shop, barber shop, beauty parlor, canteen for sundries, watch repair shop, dry cleaning and pressing shop, optometry shop, and a variety store with limited supplies of food. The stores also served as a shopping center for some non-inmates from nearby communities. The cooperative was very successful and provided rebates to inmates who had invested by purchasing shares in the enterprise.

Fire Department: Amache had a fire department with two fire engines. Staffed primarily by three shifts of inmate firefighters, the department was able to control and contain fires. There was minimal property damage and no lives lost in Amache.

Hospital: Amache's modern hospital had 150 patient beds. It included a dental clinic, surgery unit, optometry and x-ray unit, pharmacy, and sanitation facility. It was staffed with both WRA and inmate personnel. Dedicated inmate doctors and nurses received only $19 a month (less than $1 a day), while WRA personnel were paid wages comparable to persons in practice outside the camp. The discrepancy in wages was a constant source of irritation and resentment among inmate staff. It should be noted, however, that medical services provided to the inmates were excellent despite the continual turnover in key personnel who left for employment on the outside.

Newspaper: Soon after the inmates arrived, a community newspaper was started: the Granada Pioneer. Distributed twice a week, the mimeographed paper was limited in scope to camp activities, information related to relocated inmates, news of Amache men and women in military service, and editorials in both English and Japanese. The Pioneer staff was comprised mostly of inmates. There was a high turnover of staff, as many relocated to the outside.

Police Department: The important duty of preserving law and order in Amache was delegated to the Police Department. The police force was composed of three WRA internal security officers and 30 inmates who received training in proper police tactics from the WRA Chief of Security. Many of the martial arts tactics were those taught to the police chief by the head of the dojo in Denver.

Post Office: An estimated 3,000 letters and 400 packages were processed each month by the Amache Post Office. The mail was given to Block Managers for distribution.

Silk Screen Shop: A source of great pride was the Amache

Silk Screen Shop, started in June 1943. A WRA supervisor and 45 evacuees were employed at the shop. Over 250,000 training aid posters were produced for the U. S. Navy. Some evacuees who learned silk screening skills in camp then relocated and got employment doing similar work in shops on the outside.

Water and Power: Four wells were drilled at Amache. Huge pumps discharged over 400 gallons per minute of water into a 200,000 gallon storage tank. The water was chlorinated before it was pumped to various parts of the camp. Electric power was supplied by the Rural Electrification Administration.

Educational Program

A full range of educational programs was offered in the barrack classrooms of Block 8H. There were classes for all levels: nursery, kindergarten, elementary, junior high, senior high and adults. When school first started in the barracks, the level of education was poor. There were no desks or textbooks. Students sat on wooden benches, and copied what the teachers put on the chalkboard. Supplies were limited, and the curriculum was outdated. The system gradually improved.

In June 1943, a school for the senior high was completed. It included a gymnasium, science laboratory, rooms for homemaking, a library and typical offices and classrooms. The school served both high school and junior high students. The elementary school children continued to use the converted barracks in Block 8H.

The educational program was conducted in cooperation with the Colorado State Department of Education. Most of the staff were appointed by the WRA: a superintendent of schools, three principals, and 81 teachers. There were also 44 inmate assistants. Courses of study were similar to those in neighboring towns. Amache High School was accredited by the North Central Association of Colleges and Secondary Schools. In addition to the academic program, the schools offered a wide variety of extracurricular activities.

Community Governance

The central legislative body of Amache was the community council, composed of an elected representative from each of the 29 housing blocks. The 29 blocks were also divided into five districts. Each district chose a council member to serve on an executive committee; each committee was led by an elected chairperson.

The community council administered ordinances and regulations developed and issued by the WRA. A judicial commission of eight members, consisting of three WRA members and five inmate residents, conducted hearings on violations of center regulations.

Recreation and Leisure Time

Administrators knew that boredom among inmates could easily lead to problems if jobs and recreational outlets were not in abundance. To keep minds occupied and distracted, it was important to provide a comprehensive recreation program. Within the barracks, parents were worried about their children and deterioration of family unity. They were also extremely concerned about the future for themselves and their families once the camps would be closed. Their financial resources were being eroded and the camp newspaper reported continual news of hostility toward them on the West Coast, where they wanted to return to their homes and businesses.

The recreation department organized leagues and teams for young boys and girls to compete in sports such as baseball, basketball, softball, volleyball, etc. High school students organized teams and clubs similar to those on the "outside." Orchestras and vocal groups were started. Dances were held. Boy Scout and Girl Scout groups were organized. On several occasions, Amache High School teams competed with teams from nearby communities.

Amache provided a peaceful interlude for some of the elderly who had toiled in the agricultural fields and orchards of California. For the first time, some had the opportunity to develop artistic skills, to relax and converse with friends, and to pursue leisure time activities.

Leisure activities for older inmates included adult education classes for women in sewing, crocheting, weaving, knitting, dressmaking and making paper flower arrangements. Elderly men played Japanese board games, such as "goh," a favorite board game in Japan. They learned how to carve wood, to paint and to write poetry.

Special morale building events were held, such as arts and crafts festivals, agricultural fairs, 4th of July parades, camp carnivals, Obon dances, movies, talent shows, musical concerts, sports contests, sumo tournaments, and a variety of social events.

Employment in Amache

Most adult inmates found some type of job in Amache. Some worked in jobs comparable to those they had prior to camp. Others worked in jobs completely different from previous occupations. At one time Amache had a total of 3,476 inmates employed in about 25 different departments. At least one WRA employee was assigned to each department as manager or supervisor.

The salary scale for inmates was: $19 a month (less than $1 a day) for professionals such as doctors and dentists; $16 a month (about $0.80 per day) for general skill workers; and $12 per month (about $0.60 per day) for unskilled workers.

Shortage of good, efficient employees began to develop as soon as young men and women began to leave Amache for college and/or higher paying jobs on the outside. The shortage increased as men left for military service. The labor shortage was particularly evident in the farm operation as workers left camp to harvest crops on outside farms. They could earn five to 10 times more than they could in Amache. The labor problem became so acute that school children were asked to help in the agricultural harvest.

Amache Farm Agricultural Operation

The main industry of the Granada Relocation Project was agriculture. The prime objective was to produce enough vegetables and meat so that the camp would become self-sufficient in meeting the needs of the inmates. The vegetable farm and meat production operations were highly successful, despite the continual shortage of labor.

Many crops previously not grown in the area were produced on the Amache farm. These included potatoes, head lettuce, celery, spinach, lima beans, onions, tea, mung beans, daikon, etc. In addition to vegetable crops, feed crops such as hay alfalfa and sorghum were raised for chickens, pigs, cattle and other animals raised on the farm.

Surplus vegetables were occasionally sent to other relocation centers. In return, some of the other camps sent their surplus food to Amache. A vegetable canning plant was built to process some of the food. A root cellar for storing products through the winter was also built.

The farm had a completely equipped blacksmith shop for general repair of farm equipment.

The People of Amache – Displaced Americans

Two of every three inmates in Amache were American citizens, as they had been born in the United States. They were the Nisei (second generation) or Sansei (third generation). A sub-group of Nisei was the Kibei, persons born in the United States who had been sent by their parents to Japan for education in the language and culture of Japan. The Kibei were relatively few in number. Some had a difficult time when they returned to the U.S. due to limited English skills, while others made a good transition back to America.

Almost a third of the inmates in Amache were Issei, or immigrants from Japan. Some had come to the United States in the late 1800s. Most of them had come between 1900 and 1924, before immigration from Japan was stopped by the U.S. government. Since their arrival, Issei had not been allowed to assimilate into American society. Unlike immigrant groups from Europe, they could not become citizens, own land or marry persons outside their race. Opportunity for U.S. citizenship for immigrants from Japan was not granted until 1952.

Inmates could be roughly divided into two groups: urban and rural. Most of the urban residents were from Los Angeles, who had been incarcerated in the Santa Anita detention center. Most of the rural residents were from central and northern California counties who had been incarcerated in the Merced detention center.

Former occupations of Amacheans represented the full range of American workers: doctors, dentists, lawyers, engineers, teachers, farmers, day laborers, clerks, gardeners, pharmacists, fishermen, truck drivers, hotel workers, restaurant workers, government employees, etc. Some were wealthy, others were not. Brief profiles of some Amacheans are presented later in this book.

On August 27, 1942, the first inmates arrived by train from the Merced detention center. By the end of October, 1942, there were 7,567 in Amache: 4,492 from Merced, 3,062 from Santa Anita, 10 from Fresno, and 3 others. Most of the Issei men were between 60 and 70 years of age, while the women were between 50 and 60. The Nisei ranged in age from babies to 50, with an average of 18.

Military Service

Nine hundred and fifty-three men and women Amacheans volunteered or were drafted for military service. One hundred and five were wounded and 31 killed in action. It was tragic and ironic that these young men were killed fighting in Europe while their parents were still behind barbed wire in the camps in the States. They died fighting for the freedom and constitutional rights denied their parents.

Names of the men who died are carved on a granite memorial at the Amache site:

John Akimoto
Victor Akimoto
Kunio Hattori
Chikara Inouye
Frank T. Kanda
Saburo J. Karatsu
Haruo Kawamoto
Leo Kikuchi
John Kimura
Mamoru Kinoshita
Eizo Masuda
Peter S. Masuoka
Haruto Moriguchi
Akira Morihata
Kiyoshi Muranaga*
Masao Nakagaki

Ned Nakamura
Arnold Ohki
Katsunoshin Okida
Lloyd M. Onoye
Calvin T. Saito
George S. Saito
Masami Sakamoto
Masao Shigezane
Toshiaki Shoji
Robert S. Sueoka
Shigeo Tabuchi
Tadashi T. Takeuchi
Harry Tokushima
Bill Iwao Yamaji
Joe R. Yasuda

* awarded the Congressional Medal of Honor

There is a story to be told about every soldier listed above, and all others who were casualties during the war. The poignant irony of one casualty was revealed in an editorial in the *Milwaukee Journal*, dated September 15, 1944, entitled: "To Mrs. Ohki's Son."

> **Editorial**: Mrs. Yaye Ohki is a widow. She lives, with thousands of other loyal Americans, in a concentration camp – because American communities are too prejudiced and full of racial hate to accept her.
>
> Let's be honest about it – it is a concentration camp, even though it is fairly comfortable and the 'prisoners' are well treated. To call this place a relocation center is a travesty. It was meant to be that, but the refusal of most American communities to accept Japanese Americans, even after their loyalty is proved, forces them to remain in such camps, year after year.
>
> Mrs. Ohki's son, Arnold, was killed in action July 7;

the second son, Edwin, was seriously wounded; there is a third boy also in the army.

Memorial services were held in the camp for Arnold Ohki; many such services have been held for American heroes whose next of kin are forced to live in concentration camps. Arnold Ohki's mother said of her boys after Arnold's death:

"This is their country. This is their home, and my sons are working toward the betterment of their motherland and fighting endlessly to win their place in the United States as loyal citizens whose faith in America will not die, and will grow even stronger. My son Arnold proved that by sacrificing his life on the Italian front."

Do you know of any American, especially an American in so difficult a position, who has put it better?

Some Japanese Americans from Amache served in the military in Europe with the famed 442nd infantry battalion. Others fought against the Japanese in the Pacific. Still others served in the U.S. Merchant Marine and several in the U.S. Air Force. Women from Amache served with the Women's Army Corp. (WAC).

Resisters of Conscience

While most men in Amache reported for duty when they were sent notices for induction, it should be noted that some others in Amache did not respond to the draft notices for military service. They were taken to Denver at various times, brought to trial, convicted of draft evasion and sentenced to prison in Tucson, Arizona. The men said that they would be willing to serve in the Army if and when their families were released from Amache. They were "resisters of conscience." The men were eventually released after serving their time. One returned to Granada and tried to rejoin his parents, who were still in Amache. He was denied entrance, because WRA authorities did not want "trouble makers" in camp. The man had to sneak into camp after dark to see his parents. In essence, this "trouble maker" was free, while his parents, who were not "trouble makers," were still confined in camp! There were 32 Amache "resisters of conscience." After their cases were reviewed in 1947, each received a pardon from President Harry S. Truman.

100th Infantry Battalion and 442nd Regimental Combat Team

The 100th Infantry Battalion was a unit composed almost entirely of young Japanese American men from Hawaii – still considered an American territory in 1941. After extensive training in three states: Hawaii, Wisconsin, and Mississippi, the 100th was sent overseas to fight German and Italian troops in Italy and France. The men of the 100th fought with uncommon bravery and success in battle. However, they did so with such a high casualty rate they became known as the "Purple Heart Battalion." Their exploits did not go unnoticed.

On the mainland, U.S. former military and political leaders, who were formerly opposed to the enlistment of Japanese Americans serving in the military, changed their minds and approved the formation of a segregated unit; the 442nd Regimental Combat Team. Most men of the 442nd were recruited and later drafted from the concentration camps in which they had been incarcerated with their families since 1942. The 442nd received most of their training at Camp Shelby, Mississippi. The 442nd was sent to Italy to combine forces with the 100th.

Fighting primarily in Italy and France, the 442nd Regimental Combat Team became the most decorated unit for its size and length of service in American military history.

As a unit, the 442nd was awarded eight Presidential Unit Citations. The 14,000 soldiers who served with the regiment earned 18, 143 individual medals and awards:

9,486 Purple Hearts (awarded to those wounded or killed in U.S. military service)

- 21 Medals of Honor
- 52 Distinguished Service Crosses
- 1 Distinguished Service Medal
- 560 Silver Stars
- 28 Oak Leaf Clusters, in lieu of second medals
- 22 Legions of Merit
- 15 Soldiers Medals
- 4,000 Bronze Stars
- 1,200 Oak Leaf Clusters
- 12 French Croix de Guerre
- 2 Italian Medals of Military Valor

The unit suffered 9,486 casualties, including over 600 dead – over 300 percent of its original strength. As a unit, the 442nd won 43 Division commendations, 13 Army commendations, 3 Meritorious Service Unit Plaques, and 8 Presidential Distinguished Unit Citations.

NISEI Military Intelligence Service Unit During World War II

General Charles Willoughby, General MacArthur's Chief of Staff for intelligence stated that the Nisei (who served as Military Intelligence Service personnel) "shortened the war in the Pacific by two years when they enabled the Allies to learn the real strength of the Japanese Army."

Who were these Nisei and Kibei men (and women) and why were they not given the well deserved recognition provided the 100/442nd men fighting overseas in Italy and France?

Over 6,000 served in the Pacific war in every major battle against Japanese military forces. Whether it was Guadalcanal, Iwo Jima, Okinawa, the Philippines, Burma or dozens of smaller islands, the Nisei served as interrogators and interpreters of captured Japanese soldiers and sailors. The Nisei served on the front lines as cave flushers and code breakers. They used their knowledge of the Japanese language and understanding of the Japanese culture to convince enemy forces to surrender and reveal vital military information, which was used by U. S. forces to defeat the enemy.

An example: Nisei linguists were able to decipher codes used by Japanese in the Solomon Islands to learn that Admiral Yamamoto, who had planned the attack at Pearl Harbor, was flying to inspect the troops on the Solomons. They alerted the American air officials, who dispatched P-38 aircraft to shoot down the Japanese aircraft carrying Yamamoto. The P-38s pilots were successful.

A book by Joseph Harrington, *Yankee Samurai*, details several dozen similar stories of the value of the Nisei men in the Pacific. These men translated captured documents, maps, diaries, and other printed materials, such as battle plans, munitions locations, etc. One example: a document titled "Combined Fleet Secret Operations, Order No. 73," dated March 9, 1944, detailed plans for protecting the Marianas Islands against the U. S. Fleet had been captured. The document was sent to Australia, where it was translated by Nisei linguists. The information enabled Admiral Spruance to defeat the Japanese.

In 1969, the Defense Language Institute of the Presidio of Monterey, California, dedicated Nisei Hall in honor of the Japanese Americans who served in the Military Intelligence Service. Five of the buildings at the institute were dedicated in memory of outstanding individuals who served in the MIS: John Aiso, Director of Academic Training at the MIS Language School in San Francisco, and later at Camp Savage in Minnesota; Yutaka Munakata, an instructor at the MIS Language School; and three men who were killed in action fighting with the MIS: Frank Hachiya, Terry Mizutari and George Nakamura.

The exploits of the Nisei/Kibei military intelligence service was kept secret from the public for over 30 years, until 1972. U. S. military officials did not want Japanese officials to know about the Nisei linguists and their mission, or their value. The men of MIS were asked to take a vow of secrecy to not reveal their activities in the Pacific war. Finally, under the Freedom of Information Act, the lid of secrecy was lifted. Delayed recognition and military decorations for the MIS were finally given. In April, 2000, the MIS became the recipient of the President Unit Citation, the highest honor given to a U. S. military unit.

In 2010, veteran individuals of the MIS and the 100th/442nd were awarded the Japanese American Nisei Congressional Gold Medal. The Congressional Gold Medal is the most prestigious award given to civilians in the United States for achievement and contributions.

By many accounts, the Military Intelligence Service members were under-recognized for their contributions. Among the awards they did receive were:

- 56 Purple Hearts
- 428 Bronze Stars
- 9 Air Medals
- 33 Legions of Merit
- 38 Silver Stars
- 3 Distinguished Service Medals
- 1 Navy Cross
- 1 Distinguished Service Cross
- 1 Presidential Unit Citation

The following is a list of where the Rocky Mountain MIS Veterans served overseas, complied by Kent T. Yoritomo, in 1986:

Sixth Army Headquarters: fought in New Guinea, invaded the Philippines; took Manila.

Eighth Army Headquarters: fought in New Guinea, invaded the Philippines; took Mindanao.

Tenth Army Headquarters: saw its first action in the bloody battle of Okinawa.

I Corps Headquarters: landed on Luzon with the Sixth Army.

IX Corps Headquarters: unannounced until after V-J Day; headquarters were in Hawaii.

X Corps Headquarters: with the Sixth Army of Leyta.

XI Corps Headquarters: with the Eighth Army in the Philippines.

XIV Corps Headquarters: Solomon Islands and the Philippines.

XXIV Corps Headquarters: with the Sixth Army in the Philippines.

First Cavalry Division: Los Negros, Leyte, Manila.

Sixth Infantry Division: Sansapor in New Guinea, Northern Luzon.

Seventh Infantry Division: Attu, Kwajalein, Leyte, Okinawa.

Eleventh Airborne Division: Leyte, Manila, Cavite.

24th Infantry Division: New Guinea, Leyte, Corregidor, Verde Island, Mindanao.

25th Infantry Division: Guadalcanal, New Georgia, the Philippines.

27th Infantry Division: Makin Island, Saipan, Okinawa.

31st Infantry Division: Davao in Southern Mindanao.

32nd Infantry Division: Buna, Aitape and New Guinea, Leyte.

33rd Infantry Division: Baguio in Northern Luzon.

37th Infantry Division: Munda, Bougainville, Lingayen Gulf, Manila.

38th Infantry Division: the recapture of Bataan.

40th Infantry Division: Los Negros, Luzon, Panay Island in the Philippines.

41st Infantry Division: Salamaua, Marshalls, Mindanao, Palawan.

43rd Infantry Division: New Georgia, New Guinea, Luzon.

77th Infantry Division: Guam, Leyte, Okinawa.

81st Infantry Division: Anguar, Peleiu and Ulithi.

93rd Infantry Division: Morotai Island, New Guinea, Philippines.

96th Infantry Division: Leyte, Okinawa.

Americal Division: Guadalcanal, Bougainvlle, Cebu Island in the Philippines.

Far East Air Forces Headquarters: Okinawa, Ryukus Islands.

Fifth Air Force: Philippines, Southwest Pacific area.

Sixth Air Force: Caribbean area; graduates were at Calcutta.

Seventh Air Force: headquarters in Marianas, covered the Central Pacific.

Tenth Air Force: headquarters in India, covered India-Burma area.

11th Air Force: headquarters in the Aleutians, covered Northern Pacific.

13th Air Force: headquarters in Southwest Pacific; covered that area.

14th Air Force: headquarters in Chungking, covered China.

20th Air Force: Guam, Mariana Islands.

Theaters: China-Burma-India Theater, Alaskan Department, Pacific Ocean Area, Southwest Pacific Area.

Language Centers: Allied Translator and Interrogator Service, Joint Intelligence Collecting Agency, Southeast Asia Translation and Interrogation Center, Sino Translation Interrogation Center.

Other Units: Psychological Warfare, Office of Strategic Service, Office of War Information, Chinese Combat Command, MP detachments, the United States Navy, U. S. Marine divisions, British, Australian and New Zealand armies, Merrill's Marauders, Mar's Task Force.

Joint Intelligence Center, Pacific Ocean Area (JICPOA), Pearl Harbor, Hawaii.

Relocation and Resettlement

The long range goal of relocating and resettling the inmates into the mainstream of American communities began slowly as qualified persons were encouraged to leave the camps for areas outside the military exclusion zones which included all of California and parts of Oregon, Arizona and Washington. Prior to leaving Amache, inmates had to undergo a thorough investigation by the FBI and other intelligence agencies about their educational and political background. After getting governmental clearance, inmates were allowed to leave Amache and accept employment on the outside. The WRA set up field offices to assist the inmates.

Inmates were allowed to leave Amache for a wide variety of jobs. Some left to complete their college education, and others left for the military. Most relocated to Midwest and Eastern states. By the end of 1944, over 31 percent of Amache inmates had relocated to the outside. Persons remaining in Amache were primarily the elderly and families with children under the age of 18.

On January 2, 1945, the West Coast exclusion ban was lifted, and inmates were notified that they could relocate anywhere in the United States. Furthermore, they were told that the camps would be closed later in the year. The notice created much confusion and fear among the inmates still in camp. Many heads of household made plans for their return to their homes and businesses on the West Coast. Others made plans to join family members who had relocated earlier to Midwest and Eastern states.

A major concern of the inmates was safety in the resettlement process. On January 5, 1945, the Doi family of Auburn, California, returned to their home from Amache. The following is from the teletype issued by the Department of Interior to Amache officials, on January 20, 1945, to quell rumors about what happened:

> "The return was without incident until the night of January 17, when Doi heard noise in outbuilding. Investigation showed hoodlums had started small fire, which was promptly extinguished by Doi and father. Incident was reported to Sheriff's office. Following night buckshot was fired toward house from shotgun in hands of unknown person on road. Sheriff was summoned. His investigation showed several sticks of dynamite planted in packing shed. Governor Warren and State Attorney General Kenny, appraised of facts, immediately requested full protection for Doi family, followed up with

conference with Placer County Superior Court Judge, Sheriff and District Attorney who assured protection. Doi's immediate neighbors are friendly, extending help. Merchants in Auburn are cooperative. Doi family will be happier when other friends have returned to area."

The violence directed against the inmates returning to California was not an isolated incident. Some inmates found to their dismay that their homes and other buildings with all their stored possessions, had been burned. Others found their homes had been trashed and looted. Some found cemetery grave markers of their deceased had been vandalized. Many experienced insulting and derogatory remarks, although few were physically assaulted. The disturbing experiences were reported and magnified by inmates remaining in Amache. WRA administrators worked hard to counter them with photographs and accounts of inmates who had experienced positive reactions from Californians when they left Amache.

Concern for safety and other issues associated with the announced closure of the camps were shared by inmates in other concentration camps. Between February 16 and February 24, 1945, delegates from eight of the centers (Manzanar and Tule Lake did not send delegates) met in Salt Lake City to discuss the problems. Each center sent at least three delegates to represent their camps. The Amache delegates were: Sakae Kawashiri, Shinichi Furuya, and Eiji Uragami. The WRA had not sanctioned the conference, and did not provide funds for the meeting. Many of their centers had their delegates carry a set of their concerns to the conference.

Intensive discussions were held. A meeting with Dillon Myers, Director of the WRA, was arranged. He addressed the delegates on February 21, 1945. After further discussion by the delegates, a statement of facts and a set of recommendations were drawn up and sent to key governmental leaders and organizations. On the list were the following: President Roosevelt, Vice President Truman, Attorney General Biddle, Secretary of State Stettinius,

Secretary of the Interior Ickes, Secretary of War Stimson, the Speak of the House McCormick, some prominent leaders of the American Friends Service Committee like Josephine Duveneck, the American Civil Liberties Union, the Fair Play Committee, the Friends of the American Way, the American Red Cross, the Japanese American Citizens League, the YWCA, some church leaders and Judge James Wolfe of the Utah State Supreme Court.

Statement of Facts

1. Mental suffering has been caused by the forced mass evacuation.
2. There has been an almost complete destruction of financial foundations built over half a century (of life in the United States by the Japanese).
3. Especially for the duration, the war has created fears of prejudice, persecution, etc., also fears of physical violence and fears of damage to property.
4. Many Issei (average age is between 60 and 65), were depending upon their sons for assistance and support; but these sons are serving in the United States Armed Forces. Now these Issei are reluctant to consider relocation.
5. Residents feel insecure and apprehensive towards the many changes and modifications of WRA policies.
6. The residents have prepared to remain for the duration because of many statements made by the WRA that relocation centers will be maintained for the duration of the war.
7. Many residents were forced to dispose of their personal and real properties, business and agricultural equipment, etc., at a mere trifle of their cost; also drew leases for the "duration," hence have nothing to return to.
8. Practically every Buddhist priest is now excluded from the West Coast. Buddhism has a substantial following, and the members obviously prefer to remain where the religion centers.

9. There is an acute shortage of housing, which is obviously a basic need in resettlement. The residents fear that adequate housing is not available.
10. Many persons of Japanese ancestry have difficulty in obtaining insurance coverage on life, against fire, on automobiles, on property, etc.

The lengthy set of recommendations are not listed here, but they included such items as resettlement grants and loans, long-term loans, return of properties, priority from the Office of Price Administration (OPA) to obtain equipment to re-establish former businesses, establishment of hostels and other facilities, establishment of old people's homes exclusively for persons of Japanese ancestry, reinstatement of former civil service employees, release of frozen bank accounts, compensation for property loss due to fire and/or theft while in government or private storage, or during transit, and assistance in obtaining employment, including admittance into labor unions. Most of the recommendations were ignored by the WRA, and the process for closure of the camps continued as scheduled.

An attempt was made by the conference delegates to continue the dialog and have additional meetings, but the momentum was lost as the inmate population in the centers declined in number. The All Center conference in Salt Lake City was the first and only time that inmates from all of the camps were represented as a group to discuss common concerns.

By July 1945, the population in Amache had diminished to 4,292 inmates. The relocation process was accelerated, and the administration exhorted the inmates to leave. By September the population was down to 3,192 inmates. The administration made it clear that the camp would be closed in October. There would be no schools, farm, hospital or basic services.

On October 15, 1945, the final group of 126 inmates boarded the train at Granada, and left at 3 p.m. Each inmate was given $25 and a train ticket to their respective destinations. Amache was finally closed.

Camp records show that a total of 10,331 inmates had lived a portion of their lives in Amache. They included persons who had been moved to Amache from the Tule Lake and the Jerome relocation centers; some inmates from Hawaii, and some who had been in other relocation and internment centers.

There were 412 births, and 106 deaths at Amache during its three years in existence.

Registration and Re-segregation

Two major event took place in 1943 that severely disrupted the lives of inmates in the concentration camps, including Amache. In early February, teams of Army officers were sent to the camps to register inmates for military service. They had a questionnaire with a long list of questions that not only asked about basic information about the individual inmate, but also attempted to check their loyalty. Unfortunately, the officials decided to extend the registration to all adults in the camps, including females and Isseis who were at that time not allowed to become citizens. The questionnaires were labeled: Application for Leave Clearance.

Questions 27 and 28 were particularly troubling for the inmates because they were asked to respond with simple "yes" or "no" answers.

> **Question 27**: Are you willing to serve in the Armed Forces of the United States on combat duty, wherever ordered?
>
> **Question 28**: Will you swear unqualified allegiance to the United States of America, and faithfully defend the United States from any attack by foreign or domestic forces, and forswear any form of allegiance or obedience to the Japanese Emperor, or any other foreign government, power, or organization?

For many young Nisei of military induction age, the questions did not appear to pose potential problems. However, for those with families, Issei and women, there were many concerns. Some of the concerns were:

> If Isseis answered "yes" to Question 28, they would be persons without a country, since their only citizenship status was with Japan. They would only answer "yes" if the United States permitted them to become citizens.
>
> If they answered "no" to Question 28, and their children answered "yes," what would happen to the family if they were separated on the basis of their responses?
>
> Why were they being asked to respond to Question 27 when they were still being incarcerated behind barbed wire fences in a concentration camp? If they were not free, why were they being asked to defend "democracy and freedom"?

Many other concerns were expressed, and the trauma of having to answer with an unequivocal "yes" or "no" created great turmoil among the inmate population of the camps. The insensitive questions were eventually modified to make them less unsettling for the inmates, but the damage had been done. There was much distrust among the inmates about the motives of the government in requiring them to respond to the questionnaire. The turmoil and confusion among inmates caused some to respond "yes-no," "no-yes" or "no-no" or provide written explanations for their responses.

Those who responded "no-no" were considered "disloyal" and sent to the Tule Lake concentration camp in northern California. Inmates who had responded with "yes-yes" were moved from Tule Lake to other concentration camps, including Amache. On September 15, 1943, a group of 511 inmates from Tule Lake arrived at Amache, to be joined on September 22 with another 478 individuals. On September 16, a group of 125 inmates left Amache for Tule Lake.

Further discussion on the traumatic and disruptive events is available in other publications.

Life in Amache

Memories of life in Amache vary among former inmates, depending on the age at the time of their incarceration, gender, economic circumstances, pre-evacuation occupation, and in-camp experiences. To describe life in Amache is difficult, because there are always exceptions to the rule when generalized statements are made. Nevertheless, some comments will be made because some conditions and activities were experienced by all inmates.

First, there were the conditions of the barracks living. Upon arrival in a barrack apartment, inmates found a room void of furnishing except for a canvas cot, a thin cotton mattress and two wool blankets for an individual. Each room had a single light bulb in the center of the ceiling of the room, and a small black, round pot-bellied coal stove in one corner. A small coal box was near the stove. The floor consisted of a single layer of bricks, placed directly on the ground. That was all. There was no water in the barracks; consequently, there was no toilet, no sink, and no kitchen in any of the rooms.

Each room had a dry-walled ceiling, and was separated from other rooms by framing with dry-wall on one side. The exterior walls were made of 2' x 4', ¾" tongue and groove, composition material created with asphalt and small beige gravel on the outside surfaces. Later, dry-walls were provided to each room, which were cut as needed and installed by the residents. Each room had sliding glass windows, two on each side, except the smallest room, which had one on each side. There was an entry way shared by two rooms, with a door with glass inserts, and a door to each room.

Second, the inmates had to use men's and women's group toilet and shower facilities, group mess halls for eating, and a group laundry and ironing area to wash and iron their clothes. The biggest problems with the women's latrines was the lack of doors in front of each commode, and lack of any enclosure around the shower heads. Young Japanese women and girls are very modest, so shower curtains were placed in front of each commode and around each shower head for privacy. Nothing was needed for the men's commodes and shower heads, as men and boys did not need them. Many blocks bought baby bath tubs for washing infants.

Because there were approximately 250 residents in each block, there were long lines to use each of the facilities. In the morning there would be long line to use the toilets and wash basins; in the evening the lines would be for the showers. At mealtimes, there would be long lines outside the mess hall to obtain food that was served cafeteria style – without, of course, any choice of type of food. Residents then ate while sitting at wooden picnic tables with benches attached. Occasionally, when there was a shortage of food, make-do lunches or mayonnaise on rice was served. Not many would eat this type of rice, so it was often wasted.

Third, the inmates lived under a strict set of camp regulations. Freedom of movement was confined to the camp boundaries. After everyone was settled, if they needed to go outside the fence, they had to obtain a pass indicating their destination, purpose and expected time of return. Firearms, liquor and cameras were prohibited in camp, although later on the restrictions against the latter two were lifted.

Fourth, the inmates always knew that WRA appointed personnel had the final authority of approval in any important decisions affecting their lives, and were the top manager or supervisor in all camp activities. The Granada Project had three divisions: legal, report and relocation. Each division had an Assistant Project Director in charge of day-to-day operations. The major divisions were listed as 1) Operations, 2) Administrative Management, and 3) Community Management.

The Operations Division was composed of: Engineering, Motor Transport and Maintenance, Agriculture, Industry, and Fire Protection.

The Administrative Management Division consisted of: Supply

(with a Procurement Unit, Mess Hall Operations Unit, and Property Control and Warehouse Unit), Finance Section (with the Budget and Accounts Unit, and the Cost Accounting Unit), Office Services Section, Personnel Management Section, Statistics Section, and an Evacuee Property Section, which became the Relocation Section.

The Community Management Division consisted of: Education Section, Internal Security Section, Welfare Section, Health Section, Community Activities Section, Business Enterprises Section, Community Government Section, and the Community Analysis Section.

On August 20, 1942, one week before the arrival of the first group of evacuees from Merced, a detachment of 134 enlisted men and 3 officers from the 335th Military Police Escort Guard Company arrived at Amache. They were housed in their own wooden, white painted barracks in Amache, which were raised on foundations, and separated from the administrative offices and the housing of the inmates by a barbed wire fence. Administrative officials soon recognized that inmates posed no problems to the safety and security in Amache. Therefore the manned guard towers and military patrols of the camp perimeter were gradually reduced, and the tower duty was eventually eliminated. The diminished responsibilities allowed the military unit to be reduced from over 100 soldiers to 15.

A Typical Day in Amache

6 a.m. Inmates would begin to awaken. Some had risen earlier to avoid the long lines to use the toilets, showers and washbasins. Mess hall cooks had been up for several hours at this point, preparing breakfast for the inmates.

7 a.m. Mess halls throughout Amache would strike their individual bells. Inmates would line up outside and file in one at a time to receive their tray of food to eat at the picnic-type tables. Some families tried to eat as a unit,

but most did not, as family members completed morning bathroom functions at different times.

8 a.m. Many inmates went to work in the administration area with WRA camp management personnel. Others went to work on the farm. Children walked to school.

9 a.m. Women would begin work on routine chores, such as washing clothes, ironing, sewing, crocheting and knitting. Some would attend adult education classes to learn how to make artificial flowers from crepe paper; take courses on flower arranging; or learn arts and crafts. Others would work in gardens near their barracks.

Old men who did not have jobs would pass the time by playing "go," or work on garden plots, carve objects from wood, learn to sketch and paint, or converse for hours about the past, present and future.

Noon: Mess hall bells would ring for lunch. Inmates would line up again to receive their food. Inmates in the administration area and students in the schools would return to their blocks for lunch in their own mess halls. Farm personnel ate their lunches at the Koen Ranch mess hall.

The afternoon hours were similar to the morning hours: children in school, employed persons at work, mothers and the unemployed engaged in a wide variety of activities. Some went shopping at the community store, or used one of the many service enterprises in the camp (beauty shop, barber shop, shoe repair shop, optometry shop, etc.). For the sake of variety, or to obtain items not available in the coop, goods were sometimes ordered from Sears and Roebuck or Montgomery Ward through their catalogs. Many of the women sewed clothes for themselves and their daughters so that they would not all look alike.

3 p.m. Children would leave school and return to their barrack rooms. Some had homework to complete, while others played with friends. Some joined school sports or clubs, or community organizations.

6 p.m. Mess hall bells would ring again. Inmates would line up to receive their dinners. Afterwards, they would visit with friends, play sports, return to their barracks to write letters, do homework, read, play games or listen to the radio.

7 p.m. Some inmates would attend a weekly movie in one of the mess halls. Other evenings they might attend a community social event, a dance, talent show, Boy Scout or Girl Scout meeting, or an athletic event.

The routine changed when there was a sandstorm, rain or snowfall. Many activities then moved indoors; some were in the barrack rooms, the laundry area and the mess hall. Schools typically remained open.

On weekends, they could relax with friends, watch athletic events, engage in special interests and hobbies, cultivate their gardens, participate in various activities and sometimes leave the camp on a hike, a field trip, or Boy Scout overnight camping.

The Arkansas River was about five miles away and occasionally used for group picnics.

Occasionally the routine and boredom of daily life was broken by a special event, such as a center-wide carnival, agricultural fair, obon festival, or competitive sports event with center teams or teams from nearby communities. Once the high school football team challenged the undefeated Holly High football team, and won 7-0.

Some Questions Needing Answers

The most traumatic events confronted by the inmates during the evacuation, incarceration and resettlement years were:
1. The uprooting from their West Coast homes into assembly centers, and later to concentration camps;
2. The Army registration and the re-segregation of some inmates to and from the Tule Lake concentration camp;
3. The closure of some concentrations camps; and
4. Resettlement problems.

Five Questions Related to the **Uprooting of American Citizens**:
1. Why was it necessary to move Japanese Americans from their West Coast homes when they had done nothing wrong?
2. Who made the decisions, and what were the motives?
3. Why didn't the general public protest this constitutional misconduct and miscarriage of justice?
4. Why didn't the military stop the evacuation/incarceration process when they knew the tide of the war had already turned against Japan in June, 1942?
5. Why weren't the German Americans and the Italian Americans treated in the same way as the Japanese Americans?

Five Questions Related to the **Army Re-segregation of Inmates to Tule Lake**:
1. Why did authorities feel it was necessary to re-segregate the inmates?
2. Why was the questionnaire used in the re-segregation process so controversial?
3. Why did some inmates decide to give up their U.S. citizenship?
4. Why was Tule Lake selected as the location for dissidents?
5. What happened to Tule Lake inmates who chose to

stay there, rather than moving to another camp, such as Amache?

Five Questions Related to **Relocation and Resettlement**:
1. Why did the decision to close the camps create such fear, concern and confusion among the inmates?
2. What did the WRA do to assist the inmates in the relocation/resettlement process?
3. What happened at the combined relocation camp conference in Salt Lake City in early 1945?
4. Why were some inmates so reluctant to return to the West Coast?
5. Why and when did the general public change their negative attitudes toward the Japanese Americans?

Positive and Negatives of the Amache Experience

Positives

Incredible as it may seem, there were some positive parts of the Amache experience.

1. New friendships were formed. Some have lasted over a lifetime.
2. New skills were developed, although it could be said that they may have emerged as easily on the outside.
3. Older men and women had some leisure time, for the first time, to explore new areas of self-expression in arts and crafts that were virtually impossible before camp, due to previous home and work responsibilities.
4. Some who relocated to other parts of the nation discovered that there were some Americans who treated them fairly and equitably in contrast to the discrimination they had experienced on the West Coast.

Negatives

Many negative parts of the Amache experience have been expressed by former inmates. Among them:
1. Loss of freedom. The barbed wire fence, guard towers, and ever present military police who checked the entrance and exit of everyone at the main gate of Amache were constant reminders of the incarceration of the inmates.
2. Lack of privacy. Living in crowded barracks, using communal toilets and showers, eating in communal mess halls, and lacking space where one could be alone were continual problems.
3. Dust storms. Amache was on the edge of the Dust Bowl area of the Great Depression era, where terrible dust storms were frequent in the 1930s. There were days in Amache when visibility was reduced to nearly zero, which caused the schools to close once. Dust storms required indoor lights to be used, as the sky would become dark as night. Since tremendous amounts of dust entered the poorly constructed rooms, all beddings and clothes would have to be cleaned, as well as floors and furniture. Even the stoves would have to be closed, as well as the windows which would be caked with dust.
4. Poor quality of food. Before the farm was able to provide better quality and selections of foods, the inmates had problems with the beans, potatoes and bread diet originally provided daily in the mess hall; they were used to eating rice at many meals. Most of the cooks were not professionally trained cooks, so the quality of the meals varied greatly between the mess halls. Because each mess hall was allocated food based on the population of their assigned barracks, you were not welcomed at blocks other than your own, except for special occasions.
5. Poor pay. The three level pay system used to compensate the workers at Amache was a continual source of irritation. There was a great discrepancy between their pay and

those of WRA workers doing the same work, as previously explained. The top pay of $19 per month was based on paying less than a Buck Private in the Army, who received $21 per month.
6. Family deterioration. Because of communal living conditions, parents had difficulty in maintaining their traditional roles, as children spent more time with their peers than with their family, such as at mealtime. In many of the families, there was a loss of older children due to relocation to the outside and/or to military service.
7. Anxiety. Parents were anxious about the future of their families. They were worried about the deteriorating financial situation, as the government had frozen their funds, they had the loss of their homes and businesses, and needed to make many purchases for their new lives. They were uncertain of the future – where to go and what to do – when the camps would be closed.
8. Extreme climatic conditions. The inmates from the West Coast were ill prepared for the extreme heat and cold of Colorado's high desert conditions. Most had never seen snow before moving to Amache, and didn't have proper clothes to cope with the cold and wind. With limited resources, most could not purchase the proper clothing, so were glad to receive obsolete Army or Navy clothes that were issued.

Resident Inmate Stories

Many of the inmates at Amache were successful before moving to Colorado; others made noteworthy contributions later in life. The following is simply a sampling of the impact Amache residents made. They are listed alphabetically for easy reference.

Harry Akune worked in a Japanese food store in Los Angeles, and later as a gardener, prior to arriving in Amache. He volunteered for the U.S. Army, was sent to Minnesota for Military Intelligence

School, and served in the Southwest Pacific as an interrogator and translator. He was assigned to General McArthur's headquarters in Australia, and then joined the 33rd Infantry Division in New Guinea. Later, Akune was assigned to 6th Army Headquarters and then joined the 503rd Parachute Regimental Combat Team. As an intelligence specialist, he was among the first Americans to parachute into Corregidor in the liberation of that island. After the war he graduated from DePaul University with a degree in accounting. He later worked as a planning engineer.

Brush Akira Arai was a talented musician who organized his own dance band in Amache. Arai was a supervisor of warehouses in camp. Prior to evacuation, he had been manager of Sun Produce in Los Angeles, the largest wholesale produce company in the Los Angeles City Market before WWII.

Mrs. Hanan Arai was 58 years old when she arrived in Amache. Probably the oldest Nisei in camp, she was born in 1884 and had never been to Japan. Her parents operated the first Japanese boarding house in San Francisco from 1860 to 1906. It was destroyed in the 1906 earthquake. Like many older women in Amache, Mrs. Arai served as a volunteer worker and homemaker in camp.

Kaneji Domoto was an architectural draftsman in the engineering department in Amache. He had attended Stanford and U. C. Berkeley. Before evacuation, he had been a gardener/landscaper and worked on the gardens and grounds of the World's Fairs in New York and San Francisco. He studied architecture with Frank Lloyd Wright in Taliesen. As an architect and landscape designer for over 50 years, Domoto created many residential and commercial projects.

Kanetaro Domoto was one of the top nurserymen on the Pacific Coast. He started his business in 1892. His greenhouses were the largest on the West Coast. He was the first person in the U.S. to raise chrysanthemums and gardenias. He imported and introduced to the U.S., from Japan, such plants as azaleas, lilies and camellias. He did the same for peat moss from Germany, tangerines, oranges and persimmons from Holland, Belgium and Australia. From 1913 to 1920, Domoto imported over two-thirds of all plants and shrub to the U.S.

Walter Naoaki Fuchigami was a Nisei farmer from Yuba City, California, prior to arriving at Amache, where he worked as a sportswriter for the Granada Pioneer. He left the camp in 1943 to attend college in Denver. He served in the U.S. Army as an officer with the Military Intelligence Service in Japan. After the war, Walter completed a law degree from George Washington University. After jobs in Denver and Ontario, Oregon, he was appointed as an Assistant Attorney General for the State of Oregon, where he served for 19 years. He later worked in the District Attorney's Office in San Francisco.

Henry Katsumi Fujita was salesman for Electrolux Vacuum Cleaners in Sonoma County prior to his incarceration in Amache. His father, Tsuneji Fujita, was a chicken rancher who was the first Japanese American in Northern California to become legal owner of land; this was accomplished by establishing a trust for his children, who were minors, born as American citizens. He filed a lawsuit challenging the 1913 California Alien Land Law, which prohibited aliens (Japanese) ineligible for citizenship from owning agricultural land or possessing long-term leases over it, but permitted leases lasting up to three years. In 1923 the Supreme Court declared such laws constitutional. Furthermore the law was updated to make it illegal to circumvent the law as the Japanese were doing.

Robert Hamada was an elementary school student in Amache. Later in life he became a Professor of Finance and Dean of the Graduate School in Business at the University of Chicago.

Donald Hasuike was born in Burbank, California in 1929. His father was the founder of Three Star Produce Company. Over the years, George Susumu Hasuike became the owner of over 56 produce markets in the Los Angeles area prior to WWII. As a leader in the community, the father was picked up soon after Pearl Harbor and interned. In the process, he lost his chain of produce markets.

Donald, the son, his sisters and mother were incarcerated at Santa Anita and Amache before they were reunited with George, who had elected to return to Japan in a prisoner exchange on the ship Gripsholm. Donald returned to the U.S. in 1948. He completed a bachelor's degree in accounting from USC. The life history of Don is fascinating, and was captured in detail by Roy Ito for the Japanese American National Museum in 7-26-2000.

Dr. Masaichi Higaki of San Francisco was a dentist by training. Graduating from the University of California Dental College in 1910, he worked as a dentist in Amache. He was an Issei who had been living in the U.S. since 1901, when he arrived as a 20 year old from Japan. He was 63 years old, with a wife and two children when he arrived in Amache.

Dr. Benjamin Makoto Higashi was a surgeon in the Amache hospital. At age 29, he performed over 500 major operations in Amache with no fatalities. He was a graduate of Pacific Union College in Anwin, California, and received his medical degree from the College of Medical Evangelists at Loma Linda, California. After leaving Amache, Dr. Higashi joined the staff of Porter Sanitarium and Hospital in Denver. He eventually moved to Hawaii, where he served on the staff of several hospitals. His wife, Lillian Shigemi Hamaoka, was also a doctor.

Mike Honda, served as a member of Congress from 2001-2017, representing the Congressional District #15 of California. A former high school teacher, Peace Corp volunteer, a member of the Santa Clara County Board of Supervisors, and the California State Assembly, Mike was initiator of the California Civil Liberties Public Education Program. Mike was born in Walnut Creek in

June, 1941, and was interned as a young child with his family in Amache.

Florence M. Hongo, Founder and General Manager of the Japanese American Curriculum Project (JACP). As teenager, she was interned in Amache for three years. She completed a B.A. at San Francisco State University, and received a Secondary School Teaching Credential. Recognizing the need by teachers for educational materials related to Asian Americans, she started the JACP in 1969, which later became the Asian American Curriculum Project (AACP) – primary source for a vast range of educational materials on Asian Americans in the United States.

Professor Yamato Ichihashi was the most prominent scholar of Japanese ancestry in the U.S. prior to the war. He was initially at Tule Lake, and was moved to Amache for the duration of his incarceration. He was 66 years old when he arrived at Amache, and had been a professor at Stanford University since 1912. An Issei who had come to the U.S. in 1894, Ichihashi obtained degrees from Stanford and Harvard. In Amache he taught several courses for the adult education department. He also served as an unofficial adviser to the community government personnel.

Lawson Fusao Inada, professor emeritus of English at Southern Oregon University, was a young Sansei student in Amache. Prior to his arrival there, he had been in camps in Fresno, California and Jerome, Arkansas. Inada is the recipient of many honors for his poetry, including being the Oregon poet laureate. He was one of 21 poets honored at the White House for a "Salute to Poetry and American Poets."

Henry Yasanosuke Inouye was General Supervisor of the Amache Farm. He was an Issei from Courtland, and had operated and supervised general farms for large corporations in California prior to his arrival in Amache.

Chris Ishii was an animator with Walt Disney Studios. He created the lovable character of Lil Neebo and his friends, while in the Santa Anita Assembly Center before bringing them to Amache. Chris worked as a cartoonist for Amache's Granada Pioneer newspaper, prior to volunteering for the U.S. Army. He served in Merrill's Marauders in the China-Burma area, fighting against the Japanese.

Joseph Ishikawa was born in 1919 in Los Angeles. After his years in Amache, he moved to Nebraska. In 1946, he successfully organized a campaign to desegregate the Lincoln public swimming pools. His career included working as the curator of the Sheldon Museum of Art at the University of Nebraska, Assistant Director of the Des Moines Art Center, Director of the Sioux City Art Center, and at the Kresge Museum of Art at Michigan State University, where he was a full Professor.

Sakae Kawashiri was a 27 year old commercial artist from San Francisco before entering Amache. In Amache, he was in charge of the Sign Shop for the Community Enterprises. He created the logo used for Amache High School sports teams, and was elected to the Amache Community Council. He served as Chair of the Council, a position equal to "mayor," and was one of the three people to represent Amache at the all center conference in Salt Lake City in 1945.

Keisaburo Koda was one of the wealthiest Issei living in California. He was known as the "rice king" for his agricultural ventures. He pioneered the use of airplanes to plant rice, built his own mill, and established the Kokuho Rose brand.. When he returned from Amache, he found that two-thirds of his farmland and his mill had been sold (without his knowledge), his farm equipment was gone, and his hogs had disappeared. Koda persisted in starting another rice farm operation and succeeded in restoring his wealth. In Amache he was on the Board of Directors for the Consumer Enterprises.

Takashi Koga was a poultry farmer for over 20 years in Petaluma. The 41 year old Nisei was Evacuee Commission of Safety (or chief of police) in Amache.

Khan Komai was one of the editors of the Granada Pioneer. A UCLA graduate in political science, he worked as a clerk for the Los Angeles Police Department before WWII. His father was the Publisher of the Rafu Shimpo, the Japanese newspaper of Los Angeles before the war.

Ernest Kuramatsu was from Carmel Highlands. Mr. Kuramatsu was an artist, who received his training at the University of Minnesota. Born in Canada, he served six months in the Canadian Army in France during World War I. He had been working with Paul Dougherty, a famous artist of ocean water and wave paintings prior to his incarceration. In Merced Assembly Center he worked as a cook prior to arriving at Amache at the age of 58.

James Murakami was a high school student in Amache. He became an Engineer and started his own firm. He was an active leader in the JACL eventually becoming its national President. Jim married Margarette Masuoka who was also a student in Amache. Margarette became a special education teacher. The couple led the Sonoma County JACL Chapter for decades.

Peter Masuoka was active in several sports in Amache before he volunteered for the U. S. Army. He was killed in action in Europe on November 3, 1944. In high school Peter was Senior Class President, four year member of the Honor Society, member of the Executive Council, Captain of the basketball team, voted Most Valuable Player on the football team, and member of the baseball and track team. He had three brothers who also served in the Army during WWII.

Chiyoko Matsuda was a professional concert artist. A graduate of Petaluma High School, she studied voice in San Francisco, and later at the Berlin Academy of Music. She made her professional debut in Leipzig in 1936. After returning to the U.S., she performed for NBC Radio in New York and the Mutual Broadcasting Company in Seattle. Before being incarcerated in Amache, she had made over 100 public appearances on stages all over the Pacific Coast. In Amache, she worked as a receptionist in the administration building.

George Kazuyoshi Matsuura, age 36 when he arrived at Amache, was a former professional baseball player. In 1936 he had been the star pitcher for the Nagoya Giants, in Japan.

Kaye Miyamoto was transferred from Jerome to Amache before relocating to Harbert, Michigan, to work for Carl Sandburg, poet and biographer of Abraham Lincoln. He was the caretaker of the poet's pedigree goats.

Frank Yasujiro Mukaida was an Issei from Yuba City. He was paid $16 a month in Amache to capture and kill rattlesnakes. Before evacuation, he had worked as a cook in hotels and homes.

Dr. George Nagamoto was the chief of the dental clinic in Amache. A graduate of USC, he eventually became a member of the USC faculty in the College of Dentistry. A member of the American Association of Orthodontists, he was one of only two Japanese orthodontists in the world in 1942.

Ena Nakamura was supervisor of the hog farm in Amache. An Issei, he had lived in Oklahoma from 1924 to 1935 as a cowboy on a cattle ranch.

Mei Takaya Nakano was one of the first to get married while at Amache. She is the author of several books, including the folk tale Riko Rabbit, and the book: *Japanese American Women: Three Generations*. She helped organize and chaired the first Japanese American Women's Conference in Northern California. Her husband, Shiro, was trained as an interpreter with the Military Intelligence Service and served in the Pacific.

Jack Noda was a 32 year old produce grower and shipper from Denair, in central California. He was an advisor to the Stanislaus County Fair Agricultural Department, and a charter member of the Turlock Social Club. In the Merced Center he served as Commissioner of Works and Superintendent of Transportation.

Walter Oi was a blind teenager in Amache. He became a distinguished Professor of Economics at the University of Rochester. Perhaps he is best remembered for ending the draft and establishing an all-volunteer Armed Forces in the United States.

Peter K. Okada was an employee of the Los Angeles City Parks and Recreation Department prior to the evacuation. He relocated from Amache to work at Boy's Town in Nebraska under Father Flanagan. He later enlisted in the U.S. Army. After training at the Military Intelligence Service School in Ft. Snelling, Minnesota, he was sent to Manila and then Japan with the Occupation Forces. He introduced football to the Japanese, eventually becoming known as the Father of American football in Japan. After his discharge, he attended Woodbury University, graduating magna cum laude with a BBA in foreign trade. He founded and served as CEO of Alpac Foods, Inc., a company dealing in marine products.

Tom Okamoto, of Los Angeles, had been a cartoonist with Walt Disney Studios before entering Amache. He was an animator on such projects as Bambi and Dumbo, and was working on cartoon movies for the U.S. Navy and the Canadian Army when he was evacuated. In Amache, Tom worked as a high school art teacher.

Kenji Okuda was among the earliest to leave Amache. He went to Oberlin College in Ohio, where he earned a B.A. in Economics. At Oberlin he became active in student politics and was elected

Student Body President. He later received an MA from Harvard and a Ph.D. from Washington State University. After teaching at several small, liberal arts colleges, he joined the faculty at Simon Fraser University in Canada.

Dr. Masato Okuda was a dentist who had lived in Palo Alto and Santa Anita prior to his arrival in Amache. Dr. Okuda did his dental training at University of Pacific.

Arthur Okumura was born in Long Beach, California, in 1932. When Amache closed in 1945, his family moved to Chicago, where Arthur completed his elementary and high school education. He extended his education at the Art Institute of Chicago while also taking courses at the University of Chicago. Arthur painted and exhibited extensively, winning many prizes, teaching at a wide variety of colleges and universities, and having his work included in many public and private collections.

Chiyoko Sakamoto was one of only two Nisei female lawyers in the United States in 1942. A graduate of American University, she passed the California State Bar in 1939. She practiced law in Los Angeles, handling over 100 court cases. She served on the Amache legal staff.

Akira Sameshima was an active Nisei high school student in Amache. He became an engineer and worked for many years with the Army Corp of Engineers. He was an innovator devising what is now used nationally as the Simplified Design Method of processing contracts.

Masao Satow was a graduate of UCLA with an advanced degree from Princeton Theological Seminary. Active in the Japanese American Citizens League (JACL), he was elected Assistant Executive Secretary of that national organization in 1936. After being released from Amache in 1944, Satow became a national field representative for the Young Men's Christian Association

(YMCA). He continued his involvement with JACL and became their National Secretary, a position he held for 25 years. The national headquarters building in San Francisco is named for him.

Hideo (Henry) Shimizu of Petaluma, California was a 39 year old Nisei with a wife and six children when he arrived in Amache. In Petaluma he had been a successful farmer, raising chickens. In Amache he was the supervisor of the poultry farm.

Yoneko "Pat" Shimizu was born in Graton, California, on an apple ranch. After the war, she became an expert in Ikebana, the art of Japanese flower arranging. Winner of dozens of awards at the Sonoma County Fair, she gave many demonstrations of her skillful artwork in the Bay Area.

Kenichi Shintani was general manager of Consumer Enterprises in Amache. Before Amache, he had been a General Manager of Oka Produce Company in Los Angeles. Part owner of Garden Basket Markets, with 15 stores in the L.A. area, he had come to the U.S. at age 15. He completed high school and attended California Institute of Technology in Pasadena for three years.

Toshio Shoji was a foreman on an assembly plant at the Skylark Manufacturing Company in Venice, California, prior to evacuation to Amache. The company was a subsidiary of the Vultee Aviation Company, makers of a dive bomber used by the U.S. Air Force. An airplane mechanic, he maintained planes for Hollywood movie stars such as Tyrone Power, Richard Arlen, and Jean Parker. Toshio was one of many timekeepers in Amache.

Keichi "Kay" Sugahara was an orphan who grew up in a Methodist mission. A graduate of UCLA in 1932, he was very successful in the brokerage business with Universal Foreign Service. He helped organize the Nisei Week Festival in Los Angeles. He was recruited from Amache by the Office of Strategic Services (OSS), forerunner of the CIA, for propaganda work in India. His family remained in Amache until 1945. After the war, Sugawara achieved phenomenal success as a businessman. He founded and was CEO of Fairfield-Maxwell Ltd., a private company that owned and operated 45 subsidiaries with interests in oil tankers, refrigerator ships, oil and gas exploration, marine services, geophysical surveys and seismic products. He was the director of 15 business organizations in the U.S. and abroad. He chaired the U.S. Asia Institute in Washington, D.C.

Chiyoko "Pat" Suzuki, a native of Cressey, California, prior to her arrival in Amache, was a member of the Amache Junior High School Trio. The Trio won first place at the Colorado Music Festival in 1942. She was a talented singer in camp, and became a star on Broadway in her role in the musical Flower Drum Song. She appeared in television and films. The executives at RCA Victor, who held her recording contract, at one point considered her their top female vocalist, ranking alongside their three top males: Perry Como, Elvis Presley and Harry Belafonte.

Reverend Lester Suzuki was Chairman of the English Division of the Amache Christian Church. Before the evacuation, he had been a minister of the Los Angeles Japanese Methodist Episcopal Church, and helped build the first Nisei chapel in the U.S. He was a graduate of San Jose State (class of 1931), and received both bachelors and master's degrees in Divinity from Drew Theological Seminary in New Jersey.

Tagawa family of Denver. One of the top nurseries in America with over 600 employees at three locations. The family had been incarcerated in Amache in Block 7G.

After Amache they started farming in Brighton, Colorado. In 1977 they started in the horticulture business. The family enterprise built and expanded the business. They were noted for their integrity, fairness, honesty, and reliability. One of their daughters, Aiko, started the Denver Taiko group which has performed throughout the U.S.

Dr. George Y. Takeyama was the head evacuee doctor at the Amache hospital. A graduate of Stanford University, he was the first Nisei to earn a medical degree from that school in 1923. He served in World War I as a Private in the U.S. Army. Prior to his time at Amache, he served as Chief of Staff at the Los Angeles Japanese Hospital He was President of the U.S. Japanese Medical Society and Commander of the American Legion, Post 525.

Dr. Takashi Terami was a statistician and an instructor of mathematics at Amache High School. He was an Issei, arriving in the U.S. in 1910 at the age of 20, after graduating high school and one year of college in Japan. After graduating from the University of California in 1921, he received a Ph.D. in mathematics from the US. In Merced Assembly Center he was Director of Education.

Ed Tokunaga from Courtland was a teacher of agriculture in Amache. He had a bachelor's degree from Texas A & M, was an Eagle Scout, and served as Scoutmaster for Troop 162 in Amache.

Edison T. Uno was a high school student in Amache. He left the camp to be with his father in Crystal City, Texas, internment camp. Edison graduated from Los Angeles State College and attended Hastings College of Law in San Francisco. He initiated and advocated for Redress for Japanese Americans. Supported primarily by third generation Japanese Americans (Sansei), the Redress Movement gained the support of Congress and culminated in monetary compensation and an apology by U.S. Presidents Reagan and George Bush for governmental wrongdoing. In 1973, he was named by the *San Francisco Examiner* as one of its most distinguished citizens. Unfortunately, he died before Redress became a reality.

Ruth Watanabe, music librarian. Director of the Sibley Music Library of the Eastman School of Music in Rochester, New York, Ruth was identified as one of the great music librarians of the 20th century. The Sibley Library has the second largest music collection in the U.S., second only to the Library of Congress. Valedictorian of her high school class, Ruth earned BA and MA degrees in music from USC before incarceration at Santa Anita and Amache, where she taught music. She left Amache at the invitation of Howard Hanson, of Rochester University, to continue her doctoral studies at the Eastman School of Music.

Frank M. Yamaguchi was another airplane mechanic prior to arrival at Amache. A former employee of Douglas Aircraft in Santa Monica, he was their first Nisei employee, having worked for them since 1937. He left Amache in early December 1942, to work for the Curtis-Wright aviation company in Buffalo, New York.

Miki Masae Yasuhira was a registered nurse from Fresno. A graduate of Fresno State, she was one of two inmate registered nurses in Amache.

Tsuneji Yoshioka was a graduate of the University of California School of Pharmacy. Prior to Amache, he had been a pharmacist in Bakersfield, California.

This list could go on and on about the diversely talented evacuees who spent part of their lives in Amache. None should have been evacuated and incarcerated. The only thing they had in common was their Japanese ancestry, and in America that should not have been a basis for uprooting them from their homes.

Most Americans now realize the tragic error of the evacuation and incarceration. They realize that Japanese Americans are as individually different as other Americans.

Final Comments

Evacuation and incarceration were defining points for many Japanese Americans. For the elderly Issei, most of them in their late 50s and 60s, the traumatic events essentially destroyed their hopes and dreams. They felt that they were too old to start anew to rebuild their farms and businesses. For younger Issei, some returned to the West Coast, resumed their prewar lives and were successful.

For some younger Nisei, the incarceration made them vow to never again be placed in such humiliating circumstances and looked for opportunities to succeed in postwar America. Some Nisei sought anonymity and avoided identification with things Japanese, or proximity with other Japanese Americans. Some resettled in the East, South and Midwest to start new lives in new occupations. Others returned to the West Coast to resume lives interrupted by three years of life in a concentration camp.

Amache does not exist in the minds of most Americans, but for those who lived in that windswept barbed wire enclosure between August 1942 and October 1945, the memories remain vividly alive.

Amache occupied a unique time and place in American history. Amache should be remembered as a symbol of what can go wrong, even in a democracy, when racist ideas replace rational thinking in the minds of its citizens.

Military necessity was the false rationale used to remove a single group of American citizens from their home and occupations. No attempt was made to determine the Japanese Americans' loyalty to America. No charges of espionage or sabotage were ever filed against Japanese Americans, simply because no such activities took place within the group. Simply stated: our government ignored the constitutional rights of this group of citizens. By using the term "non-aliens," instead of U.S. citizens or Americans, during the evacuation and incarceration period, our government officials deliberately misled the public and kept them from opposing this blatant travesty of justice.

In addition, the alien Japanese Americans were extremely law-abiding and industrious. They were contributing members of their communities, with no record of any subversive activities. Yes, they were incarcerated for no reason other than their race. They were not treated the same as the German and Italian aliens in America. Competition and greed were the ugly reasons for their incarceration. They simply looked different to other Americans, so were easy to "get rid of" from the West Coast.

Freedom and justice for all Americans were the fundamental issues tested during this period, and Japanese Americans were the victims of governmental wrongdoing. A fundamental question is posed: Can it ever happen again? And if so, which group of Americans will be targeted next time?

Summary: Who, What, Where, When and Why

The evacuation and incarceration of Japanese Americans during WWII

Who: Americans of Japanese ancestry. There were only about 126,000 persons (about one tenth of one percent) in the United States mainland. Of this number, about 112,000 lived in California, Oregon, and Washington. Before the war, they were small businessmen, farmers, students, housewives, artists, doctors, dentists, nurses, etc. They were law abiding, loyal, productive American citizens, neighbors, and friends.

What, Where and When: Between December 1941 and March 1946, almost all people of Japanese ancestry living in California and parts of Washington, Oregon and Arizona were evacuated and incarcerated for varying lengths of time (several months to three and a half years) in assembly centers, relocation centers, and detention facilities such as jails or prisons, and/or internment camps. While the term "concentration camp" was not officially used, the term was freely used by observers and politicians who were aware of the actions of our government during that period. The relocation/concentration camps were erected in remote and desolate areas of Arizona, California, Colorado, Utah, Wyoming, Idaho and Arkansas.

The United States was not alone in evacuating and incarcerating those of Japanese ancestry. Canada did the same thing, as did many South American nations, such as Peru. The Peruvians were sent to internment camps in the U.S. at the request of the U.S.

government. The Peruvians were needed as exchange personnel for American POWs. In Alaska, the Aleutian Islanders were evacuated and incarcerated in abandoned fishing and mining camps in Southwest Alaska during WWII. Housing and living conditions for the Aleuts were deplorable and life threatening; many died.

Eventually, some evacuees in the relocation/concentration camps were permitted to leave the centers for employment or continue their education in communities and colleges in eastern or Midwestern states. Many Japanese Americans volunteered or were drafted into the Army to fight in Europe and/or the Pacific.

Why: Seven primary reasons are listed: racism, fear, ignorance, greed, media inaccuracy and distortion, political opportunism, and public apathy.

1. **Racism.** There had been a long history of racial prejudice against Japanese and Japanese Americans at the national, state, and local levels. At the national and state levels, it took the form of discriminatory legislation, such as laws forbidding citizenship, ownership of land, and intermarriage. In 1924, the government passed legislation that virtually stopped all immigration from Japan. In many communities, it took the form of segregation in housing and cemeteries, and no admittance to swimming pools, golf courses, social clubs and organizations. In a few communities there were segregated schools.
2. **Fear.** There was widespread fear by the public that Japan would invade the West Coast. The fear was based on hysteria generated by unsubstantiated newspaper reports about rumored air attacks and false sabotage activities.
3. **Ignorance.** Most Americans did not know persons of Japanese ancestry socially or economically. They did not go to the same churches, social events, or interact on an informal basis. While their children went to the same schools, social interaction was limited. The public was unaware that U.S. children, who had Japanese-looking

faces, spoke little or no Japanese, and had entirely American social values and habits.
4. **Greed**. In 1940, Japanese Americans owned or leased considerable acreage growing fruits, flowers, and vegetables in West Coast states. The land owned by the Japanese Americans was in the names of the children of parents ineligible for citizenship and denied land ownership. Envious and greedy white Americans saw an opportunity to acquire the land, businesses, and properties at bargain basement prices. They were successful beyond their wildest dreams!
5. **Media inaccuracy and distortion**. Hollywood films depicted the Japanese as wicked, sly, and sinister villains. No positive images were presented. Newspapers were particularly hostile toward Japan and Japanese. No distinction was made to differentiate Japanese in Japan from American citizens of Japanese ancestry, like they did with the Germans ("Nazis") and Italians ("Fascists"). In fact, when military orders were issued to evacuate the Japanese Americans, no mention was made that these persons were American citizens. Only the terms "alien" and "non-alien" were used! The public was never informed that the persons targeted for evacuation were American citizens!
6. **Political opportunism**. Political opportunism was rampant. At the national level it was evident in the actions of President Franklin D. Roosevelt and some members of his cabinet. At the state level, it was evident in the actions of military leaders such as General John L. DeWitt and Colonel Karl Bendetsen; and politicians such as Earl G. Warren, Attorney General of California and later Chief Justice of the Supreme Court. At the local level, politicians echoed the sentiments of the higher level officials.
7. **Public apathy**. Public apathy played a major role in what transpired. The public simply did not care that their friends and neighbors of Japanese ancestry were getting

their Constitutional rights trampled on. As long as it was not happening to them, they simply ignored it. Except for the American Friends Service Committee and individuals such as Robert G. Sproul, President of the University of California, few voices were raised to protect the injustices being perpetrated upon the Japanese Americans.

Governor Ralph Carr

Governor Ralph Carr of Colorado was the only political official in the western states in 1942 who indicated an understanding of the evacuee's dilemma in being forced from their homes with no acceptable place to go for relocation and resettlement. His moral courage and compassionate willingness to accept the Japanese Americans to Colorado was punished by the voters in the next election, and basically destroyed his political career. Ironically, in 2000 he was selected as Colorado's Man of the Century by the Denver Post for his courageous stand. In April 1942, Carr was one of ten western state governors who met in Salt Lake City with Eisenhower and his WRA staff to discuss proposals for relocating the evacuees from the West Coast. While all other governors resisted and rejected the proposals, Governor Carr made the following statement:

> "If we do not extend humanity's kindness and understanding to these people (evacuees), if we deny them the protection of the Bill of Rights, if we say they may be denied the privilege of living in any of the 48 states, and force them into concentration camps without hearing or charge of misconduct, then we are tearing down the whole American system. If these people are not to be accorded all the rights and privileges which the Constitution gives them, then those same rights and privileges may be denied to you and me six months from now for another just as poor reason as the one which is now offered against the Japanese."

Source: Foote, Caleb, "Outcasts! The Story of America's Treatment of Her Japanese American Minority." *Fellowship Magazine*, a publication of the Fellowship of Reconciliation, 1944

In Remembrance of Those Internees Who Died in Amache

Araki, Kanzo
Baba, Tomi
Domoto, Kentaro
Eda, Ayame
Eijima, Keiichiro
Emi, Hisakichi
Fujiu, Shoko
Fukusawa, Tameshiro
Furumoto, Isono
Goda, Kennosuke
Homma, Kyushiro
Honda, Kazumi
Horiuchi, Giichi
Ishizu, Fuji
Ito, Emiko
Ito, Masagoro
Ito, Shikio
Iwasa, Mura
Kajiwara, Kuniko
Kasai, Ai
Kawamura, Ryosuke
Kawano, Haruko
Kawasaki, Kanemasa
Kawase, Kichitaro
Kimoto, Hannosuke
Kitagawa, Mitsu
Koda, Matsukichi
Koyama, Komakichi
Kubo, Fusako
Kunisaki, Kiyo
Marufuji, Nemokichi
Marumoto, Kikujiro
Matsuda, Yosuke
Matsuda, (infant)
Matsushita, Iwagoro
Mayeda, Goichiro
Mitani, Tsu
Miyamoto, (infant)
Miyano, Tamano
Miyazaki, (infant)
Mizutani, Masaemon
Mori, Tokichi
Morimoto, Nobuko
Morioka, Fumio
Murakami, Masamichi
Murakami, Motome
Muramoto, Kiyoshi
Nagai, Ssaichiro
Nakamoto, Tamakichi
Nakamura, Toyajiro
Nakamura, Tsuya
Nakane, Yunosuke
Nakanishi, Hidemitsu
Namura, Haru
Namura, Raku
Noda, Grace
Noguchi, Taneko
Nomura, Biwa
Oda, Sohei
Odama, Riye
Ogata, Tomoki
Ohama, Umesuke
Okamura, Hiroshi
Oki, Katsuji
Okimoto, Asayo
Okuhara, Tora

One, Sosuke
Oniki, Fuji
Oshita, Kanichi
Ota, Akihito
Ota, Miyo
Otani, Matsukichi
Sato, Roku
Sato, Ryozo
Shiina, Tatsunsuke
Shimosaka, Iwakichi
Sonoda, Kikuzo
Sotomura, Kosaburo
Sugawara, Hideji
Sugioka, Isamu
Sugita, Yoshishige
Sugiura, Kasakichi
Sumi, Isao
Sumimoto, Shinsuke
Takata, Tokujiro
Takemoto, Gosaburo
Takemura, Paul
Tamura, Steven
Tani, Yasujiro
Tanita, Eikichi
Tanizawa, Nakanobu
Toyama, Haru
Tsutsui, John Paul
Tsutsui, Shigeo
Ugi, Kimi
Umezawa, Toku
Uyeda, Mario
Uyemoto, Mitsuru
Uyemoto, Tomiko
Wada, Shizuno
Watanabe, Kohei
Yama, Suyekichi

Yamada, Tosaburo
Yamaguchi, Iwami
Yamamoto, Yachio
Yamamoto, Yasue
Yamanaka, (infant)
Yamasaki, Kichisuke
Yokoyama, Kuni
Yoshihara, Eii
Yoshimoto, Eikichi
Yoshimura, Arakichi
Yoshioka, Masano
Yoshioka, Kiyo

Total: 114 Persons

*Translated from Japanese by Nobuo Furuiye and Sadako Tsubokawa of Denver, CO

Two Mysteries in the History of the Amache Camp

THERE ARE TWO MYSTERIES associated with Amache.

The first is how Lloyd Onoye, a Japanese American soldier with the 442nd was listed as killed in action on the granite memorial at the Amache grave site and also listed on a memorial at the Poston Camp.

The second mystery is about a claim in a book (*Wounded Tiger*), published in 2014, which mistakenly states that a group of Japanese Navy prisoners of war were placed and treated for unspecified wounds in Amache. According to Martin Bennett, author of the book, the POWs included an officer named Kanegasaki, who had survived the sinking of the carrier Hiryu during the battle at Midway.

The book also mentions Margaret (Peggy) Covell Struble, a young woman who worked as a social worker in Amache, Jacob DeShazer, a crew member of a plan led by Colonel James Doolittle on the mission to bomb Japan in mid-April 1942, and Captain Mitsuo Fuchida, the lead pilot of the Japanese Naval attack at Pearl Harbor.

The first mystery began when an article appeared in the Watsonville JACL newsletter. The article was written by Rudy Tokiwa, who lived in the camp in Poston, and Judy Niizawa, who lived in Amache. Rudy was a close friend of Lloyd Onoye. Both volunteered from Poston Camp. Both were assigned to the 442nd Infantry Regiment. Onoye was killed in action in Italy. Tokiwa was severely wounded, but survived the war. Lloyd Onoye's parents had moved from Poston to Amache to be with their eldest son Charles. The U.S. Army informed Lloyd's parents, both in Amache at the time, about his death. This explains how his name appears on the Amache memorial. The fact that Lloyd had lived and volunteered from Poston explains how his name also appears at the Poston memorial. Lloyd is buried at Arlington Cemetery.

The second mystery is more complex, and took over two years to resolve. Martin Bennett had written a screenplay and then a book titled *Wounded Tiger*, about Captain Fuchida's conversion to Christianity from Buddhism due to two events: One, an encounter with a longtime navy friend Kanegasaki, who had survived the sinking of aircraft carrier Hiryu, and supposedly met Covell in Amache in 1945. She was a missionary's daughter who had grown up in Japan. When war between Japan and the U.S. became imminent, the parents sent Peggy and her siblings to the U.S. The parents moved to the Philippines. The parents were eventually found by Japanese forces and beheaded.

Peggy learned about her parents' death while attending Keuka College in New York. Following a period of anger, she remembered meeting two students attending Keuka who told her about their camp experience in Minidoka. After graduating from Keuka, she decided to help Japanese Americans in the camps as an act of forgiveness. She applied for work with the WRA, was accepted, and assigned to the Granada Relocation Center (Amache).

The second event was triggered by Jake DeShazer, who had survived capture and torture by the Japanese military, and forgave his enemies based on his Christian beliefs. He returned to Japan after the war as a missionary, met Fuchida, and was instrumental in converting the former pilot to Christianity.

After reading *Wounded Tiger*, a group of us who had been interned at Amache knew that Japanese Navy POWs were never at Amache. We began corresponding with Bennett to correct his error in placing POW Kanegasaki and meeting with Covell in the camp. As expected, Bennett resisted saying it was up to us to

provide accurate information to counter his claim in the book. We were able to find conclusive information from a variety of sources:
Three key pieces of evidence are:

1. Kanegasaki and his Hiryu shipboard survivors were captured, and interrogated at Midway Island, Pearl Harbor, and San Diego, were sent to Camp McCoy in Wisconsin in November 1942. McCoy was the only camp for Japanese POWs in the U.S. for many years. In his book *Anguish of Surrender*, author Ulrich Straus (p. 206) reported that the officers at Camp McCoy were transferred to Camp Kennedy Alien Detention Camp in Texas in late Spring 1945. While the officers were unnamed, it seems certain that Kanegasaki was among the three persons transferred. This information indicated the whereabouts of Kanegasaki during the time Covell was in Amache. Covell left Amache on July 27, 1945, for a job with the YWCA in Bridgeport, Connecticut.
2. Bill Creech, archivist with National Archives and Records Administration, in a phone conversation and follow up letter to Fuchigami, stated: "There were no Japanese POWs held at the War Relocation Authority Camp Amache."
3. Douglas Shinsato, translator of the book on Fuchida titled *For That One Day*, provided an article on November 27, 2017, titled "Captain Mitsuo Fuchida – Leader of the Attack on Pearl Harbor," with two notable quotes related to Peggy Covell. Shinsato says that Covell's sister, Alice Covell Bender, wrote: "Peggy had nothing to do with Japanese POWs."

The second, and more important, was a letter from Peggy Covell Struble to Reverend Yoshio Oshima, dated August 11, 1976. She wrote: "The late Capt. Fuchida tried to establish the facts of my U.S. Government work, but I'm afraid he never got the facts straight. The persons of Japanese ancestry were moved from their homes on the West Coast of the U.S.A. as you know, and my "tsumaranai" (humble, insignificant) work was only with individuals and families at the Granada Relocation Center in Colorado."

The evidence provided to Bennett convinced him of his error about Covell meeting Kanegasaki in the camp called Amache.

Remembering Amache: Past, Present and Future

Over the years, Amache has progressed from a listing on the National Register of Historic Places in 1994, to designation as a National Historic Landmark in 2006. In 2014, a Colorado House Resolution 14-1017 was adopted by both the Senate and House to Recognize Amache's Twentieth Anniversary on the National Register of Historic Places. In 2018, a bill (S.2870) was introduced in Congress to conduct a study to examine the feasibility of Amache becoming a National Park. In 2019, the bill became part of an omnibus land management bill signed by the President. A progress report on the future development of the Amache site is available at www.Amache.org.

Many organizations have been involved in remembering Amache:

- **Amache Preservation Society** (APS). Based in Granada, Colorado, near the Amache site. It was started in the 1990s by John Hopper, a history teacher and principal at Granada High School. He and his students have been key to the preservation and restoration of Amache by maintaining the site, making presentations about Amache to schools in Kansas, Colorado, and Oklahoma. They even made a presentation in Japan. In Granada, the group started a museum, gathering artifacts, purchasing books, giving tours of the Amache site, writing a newsletter, and constructing a model map of the camp. APS was also heavily involved in restoration efforts involving the water tower, guard tower, barrack and recreation building now in place on the Amache site. The Amache Museum is now the main tourist attraction in the town of Granada.

- **Amache Historical Society** (AHS). Based in Los Angeles, led by Minoru ("Min") Tonai. Another key support organization, it is composed primarily of former residents of Amache. The group has been a financially and historically supportive group with many reunions over the years, with half of their profits given to the Amache Preservation Society. In 1998, they organized the largest return to Amache, a reunion with over 600 people in attendance. With most former Amacheans over the age of 80, the leadership has passed to Amache Historical Society II.
- **Amache Historical Society II**. Based in Seattle, it is led by Frances Palmer. This group is composed of third, fourth and fifth generation Japanese Americans who parents and grandparents were in Amache. They meet periodically in Los Angeles, produce an informative newsletter and maintain the www.Amache.org website.
- **Amache Club**. Based in Denver, this group was the successor of the Denver Optimist Club. They used to organize the annual Amache pilgrimage and support the Amache Preservation Society in Granada with financial and material assistance. The group has unfortunately dwindled in membership and has become unable to continue its financial assistance to the Granada group. The core activities of this group have been transferred to the Japanese American Association of Colorado.
- **Friends of Amache**. Based in Denver, this group original formed in response to the National Parks Service (NPS) grants program, whereby various individuals and organizations could apply for grants to fund projects. Friends of Amache serves as an umbrella organization so that duplication of request to NPS would be avoided and proposals would be in line with the development and management plan agreed upon by Amache stakeholders with NPS in 2006. Results of the meeting were published

as the Granada Relocation Center (Amache) National Historic Landmark Comprehensive Interpretive Plan and Conceptual Plan. A summary of the plan is included as an Appendix in this book.

- **Japanese American Association of Colorado**. This group has been in existence over 100 years, serving the Japanese American population in Colorado with a wide variety of activities. Recently it replaced the Amache Club and took on the responsibility for organizing and funding the annual pilgrimage to Amache.
- **Denver University Anthropology Department**. Dr. Bonnie Clark began working in 2005 to design and develop a collaborative project with a variety of people and organizations interested in Amache. The project was to combine archaeological on-site research with stakeholders such as the Amache Preservation Society, the town of Granada, and especially former internees, who lived in Amache. Dr. Clark has conducted a field camp at the Amache site to study artifacts found by her students and former internees. Information from the research has been used to develop informative presentations to the public. The field camp is held biennially and has attracted many former internees and/or their descendants. A newsletter has been developed for distribution to interested parties.
- **JACL Mile High Chapter**. This group has helped disseminate information about Amache and provided some funding for preservation activities. The chapter has helped organize such items as an EO 9006 Remembrance Day commemoration conducted at several venues in Denver.
- **Colorado Preservation, Inc**. This organization has been heavily involved in restoration efforts at Amache. They have written and received grants which have made it possible to rebuild the water tower, reconstruct a guard tower and a barrack, and move a recreation barrack from Granada to its original site at Amache.

- **National Park Service** (NPS). NPS has awarded grant monies for several projects at Amache, such as the rebuilding of the water tower, reproduction of a guard tower, move of a former recreation barrack, and reproduction of a barrack. They have also conducted meetings resulting in a comprehensive plan for the development and management of the Amache site. See a summary of the planning in the Appendix.
- **Colorado History Museum** and the **City of Aurora Museum** have developed exhibits on Amache. The Aurora History Museum exhibit on Amache was opened on July 27, 2010 and closed on October 31, 2010. The Colorado History Museum exhibit on Amache opened in 2012 and closed in 2020. The exhibit included a video, some artifacts, and an oversized replica of a typical barrack "apartment" room.
- **DENSHO**. This organization, based in Seattle, was started by Tom Ikeda and has become one of the major sources of information about the entire exclusion/incarceration experience. The organization has video-interviewed hundreds of former inmates, including those who were in Amache.
- **Amache.org**. This website is the best source for gaining information about past, current and future activities related to Amache. While the basic facts about the Amache site do not change, additional information is uncovered through artifacts found by archaeological work done by Denver University students at Amache and through interviews with former inmates.
- **The National Park Conservation Association.** Tracy Coppola. This group has been strongly supportive of the preservation and restoration activities at Amache. The camp is among the top priorities of the group.
- **Granada**. The town of Granada has become actively involved in assisting the Amache Preservation Society in the preservation and restoration activities. Since the

town owns the camp site, it is critical that such support be secured. Reciprocally, the town benefits financially from its proximity to the Amache site, the museum and research facility, and the increased visibility as a tourist attraction in the area.

Pilgrimages and Reunions

There is an annual pilgrimage to Amache on the third Saturday of May. It is a full day schedule of events beginning with a long bus ride from Denver to the Amache site, a memorial service at the cemetery lunch and program at Granada High School, the choice of a visit to the Amache site or a visit to the Amache museum, and another long bus ride back to Denver.

Amache reunions have been sporadic and held in various locations. The first was in Denver in 1975, organized by Russell Endo and Marge Taniwaki. Others have been held in San Francisco, Los Angeles, Las Vegas, Sacramento, Reno and Colorado Springs. The Denver and Colorado Springs reunions included visits to the Amache site. The 1998 reunion, held in Colorado Springs, was attended by over 600 people. Min Tonai and the Amache Historical Society organized almost all the reunions.

On Executive Orders – Then and Now

On February 19, 1942, President Franklin D. Roosevelt signed EO 9066 (in the absence of martial law), to allow the military to evict and incarcerate over 112,000 people of Japanese ancestry – aliens and American Citizens, from their homes, farms and businesses. On February 19, 1976, President Gerald R. Ford terminated EO 9066 in a Proclamation addressed to the American public. While it appears that such a travesty of injustice perpetrated on Japanese Americans will probably never be repeated against them, many Executive Orders in existence can be used against other Americans. Consider the following Presidential EXECUTIVE ORDERS listed on the FEDERAL REGISTER:

EO 10990 Allows the government to take over all modes of transportation and control of highways and seaports.

EO 10995 Allows the government to seize control of all communications media.

EO 10997 Allows the government to take over all electrical power, gas, petroleum, fuels, and minerals.

EO 10998 Allows the government to take over all food resources and farms.

EO 11000 Allows the government to mobilize civilians into work brigades under government supervision.

EO 11001 Allows the government to take over all health, education, and welfare functions.

EO 11002 Designates the Postmaster General to operate a national registration of all persons.

EO11003 Allows the government to take over all airports and aircraft, including commercial aircraft.

EO11004 Allows the Housing and Finance Authority to relocate communities, build new housing with public funds, designate areas to be abandoned, and establish new horizons for populations.

EO11051 Specifies the responsibility of the Office of Emergency Planning and gives authorization to put all Executive Orders into effect in times of increased international tensions and economic or financial crisis.

EO 11310 Grants authority to the Department of Justice to enforce the plans set out in Executive Orders, to institute industrial support, to establish judicial and legislative liaison, to control all aliens, to operate penal and correctional institutions, and to advise and assist the President.

EO 11049 Assigns emergency preparedness function to federal departments and agencies consolidating 21 operative Executive Orders issued over a 15 year period.

EO 11921 Allows the Federal Emergency Preparedness Agency to develop plans to establish control over the mechanisms of production and distribution, of energy sources, wages, salaries, credit, and the flow of money in U.S. financial institutions in any undefined emergency. It also provides that when a State of Emergency is declared by the President, Congress cannot review the action for six months.

These Executive Orders date back to John F. Kennedy. Jimmy Carter signed a major consolidation of Executive Orders which gives control to the Federal Emergency Management Agency (FEMA). If Martial Law is implemented in the United States, it would only take a presidential signature on a proclamation and the Attorney General's signature on a warrant, to which a list of names is attached. The type of crisis which could trigger Martial Law in the U.S. include:

- Threat of imminent nuclear war.
- Rioting in several U.S. cities simultaneously.
- A series of natural disasters which affect a widespread danger to the populous.
- Massive terrorist attacks.
- A depression in which millions are unemployed and without financial resources.
- A virus pandemic.
- A major environmental disaster.
- A combination of errors in the use of weapons of mass destruction.

>Source: "The Reality and Truth of FEMA Concentration Camps across America." There is one photo: Amache, Colorado.

Executive Orders continue to be issued. Dylan Mori, board member of the Mile High JACL Chapter listed several in the January-February 2017 newsletter:

EO 13767 Authorizes the construction of a wall on the border between the United States and Mexico.

EO 13768 Increasing resources for immigration and deportation law enforcement in the U.S. It requires cities to comply with and provide the federal government with information on the immigration status of their residents, with the threat of blocking federal aid and funding to "sanctuary cities" which refuse to comply with this order. The Attorney General would additionally publish reports on the immigration status of any people incarcerated for crimes in both federal and state prisons.

EO13769 A ban on all refugees and visa holders from several Middle Eastern and African countries, including: Iran, Iraq, Libya, Somalia, Sudan, Syria, and Yemen. Additional countries may be added by the President. The countries listed are majority Muslim, and the order notes that refugees who are of a "minority religion in the individual's country of nationality (i.e., non-Muslim) will be given priority for entry into the U.S. This EO has already been used against persons with visas and green cards from the above listed countries to detain them at airports.

There are other EOs and memorandums that have had, or will have, an impact on the lives of Americans here and abroad. EO 9066 is not forgotten by most Japanese Americans.

In 2014, at the University of Hawaii, the late Supreme Court Justice Antonin Scalia reminded us:

"You are kidding yourself if you think the same thing will not happen again. In times of war, the laws fall silent."

Who will be the future targets for such exclusion and incarceration? Which Executive Orders will be sued to implement the actions?

A Key Question Answered

ONE OF THE TROUBLING QUESTIONS that lingered in the minds of many who were in Amache and other camps was: Who put us into them? Was it President Roosevelt, who signed EO 9066? Was it the military, headed by General DeWitt? Was it someone else, like Earl Warren, Walter Lippman, John McCloy, Colonel Bendetsen, etc.?

In 2004, a new book appeared titled: *The Colonel and the Pacifist*. The author, Klancy Clark deNevers, grew up in Aberdeen, Washington with Karl Bendetsen. Professor Roger Daniels, who authored many books about the Japanese Americans and the incarceration during WWII wrote: "neither I, nor any of the numerous other scholars, took a hard look at Bendetsen's past." Kai Bird said: "A chilling tale of Mendacity and crass ambition… a painful reminder of how ignorance and war hysteria made it possible for one man to trample on the Constitution." The book details the nefarious actions of the young Colonel's history.

Since publication of the book, others have appeared, such as *INFAMY* in 2015, by Richard Reeves. He characterized Lieutenant General John DeWitt and Colonel Karl Bendetsen as: "both bigots, the former a fool, the latter a pathological liar." Reeves also points out that in the 1944 entry of *Who's Who in America*, Bendetsen says he "conceived the method, formulated the details, and directed the evacuation of 120,000 persons of Japanese ancestry from military areas." Reeves also reports that "when the Japanese evacuation was being investigated by a Congressional Committee in the 1970's, Bendetsen was asked about his involvement, and he replied, 'of course, I wasn't in high level meetings, I was only a Major.' This big lie was an attempt to avoid accountability for his actions."

The following entry will provide additional information about Bendetsen.

Colonel Karl Robin Bendetsen: the Man Who Put Us in the Camps

Scholars who have written books about the exclusion/incarceration period identified many individuals and organizations who advocated for the tragedy which occurred: President Franklin D. Roosevelt (FDR), who signed Executive Order 9066; General DeWitt, who was assigned to carry out the military order; Attorney General of California, Earl Warren; the Native Sons of the Golden West, California State Grange, American legion, Walter Lippman, John McCloy, Karl Bendetsen and countless others.

While most of those involved eventually realized the errors of their actions, and apologized for them, three of the more prominent people did not: Walter Lippman, John McCloy and Karl Bendetsen. While brief statements will be made about Lippman and McCloy, this section will focus primarily on Colonel Bendetsen, who proudly admitted to being the architect, advocate and administrator of "assembly centers" used to house the Japanese Americans while more permanent "relocation centers" were being built.

Lippman. Reeves (p. 49) wrote that Walter Lippman was "the most respected newspaper columnist in the nations' capital. He had dinner with (Earl) Warren and Percy Heckendorf, the District Attorney of Santa Barbara County. Heckendorf said Lippman wrote almost word for word what Warren told him." The following article appears in the *Washington Post*, the *New York Herald Tribune*, and 250 other newspapers on February 13, 1942:

"The Pacific Coast is in imminent danger of a combined attack from within and without ... It is a fact there has been no important sabotage on the Pacific Coast. From what we know about Hawaii and about the 5th column in Europe, this is not as some would like to think, a sign there is nothing to be feared, it is a sign that the blow is well organized and that it is held back until it can be struck with maximum effect."

We now know that this was false information.

The article was extremely influential. FDR had it circulated to key advisors. All members of Congress from California, Oregon and Washington signed a letter to FDR on the following day, saying: "We recommend the immediate evacuation of all persons of Japanese lineage and all others, aliens and citizens alike, whose presence shall be deemed dangerous or inimical to the defense of the United States from all strategic areas." Five days later, FDR signed EO 9066.

McCloy. Reeves notes that *Harper's* magazine called McCloy "the most influential private citizen in American history." McCloy advised eight Presidents, from FDR to Reagan. His biographer, Kai Bird, wrote in his book *The Chairman*:

"More than any other official, McCloy was responsible for the internment of the entire Japanese American community inside barbed wire camps for three years. His arguments had carried the day against the Justice Department's constitutional concerns. He had allowed the early relocation program to evolve into a policy of forcible internment. And he had repeatedly made it possible to prolong the internment for political reasons long after any military justification for the action existed. Had it not been for his careful legal defense of the War Department's policies, the Supreme Court might well have declared the entire enterprise unconstitutional."

(Chapter 8, *Internment of the Japanese Americans*, p. 292.)

McCloy never apologized for his actions.

Bendetsen. Wikipedia has a lengthy profile on Colonel Bendetsen. A book by Klancy DeNevers, *Colonel and the Pacifist*, is an excellent source of information on him.

Bendetsen was born on October 11, 1907, to Albert and Anna Bendetson. Both had parents who came as Lithuanian Jewish immigrants. The Bendetsons moved to Aberdeen, Washington. Karl Bendetson was a grandson of Lithuanian Orthodox Jews. However, he changed his name to Karl Bendetsen on February 4, 1942, and later claimed to be of Danish origin. Why? Richard Reeves, in his book *Infamy* (p. xvi), described Karl Bendetsen as a "brilliant pathological liar." Did Bendetsen conceal his family origin because his actions in the evacuation and incarceration resembled Hitler's activities against Jews in Europe and might be raised in later accountability sessions?

Japanese Americans will always remember that it was Bendetsen who said to Father Lavery, of the Maryknoll Center in Los Angeles, who was in charge of an orphanage with children of Japanese ancestry, which children should be sent to camp. The Colonel's comment was: "I am determined that if they have one drop of Japanese blood in them, they must go to camp." Reeves describes Bendetsen's racist tendencies in his book *Infamy* on pages 44 to 48.

How did Bendetsen, as a staff officer with the rank of Major, in the office of Provost General Gullion in Washington, DC, gain such power? Bendetsen, a Stanford law graduate, was assigned to study the status of aliens in the U.S. He was particularly good in drawing up legal documents, which could be used to incarcerate foreign born aliens, if necessary.

When war began in December, 1941, his background and experience was deemed invaluable, and he was assigned to assist General DeWitt on the West Coast to deal with military matters related to the Japanese and Japanese Americans. Confronted with carrying out the directives of EO 9066, Secretary of War Simpson passed the buck to his Chief of Staff (McCoy), who passed it on to General DeWitt, and ultimately to Bendetsen. Bendetsen's goal was to become a general, and used the opportunity to evict and incarcerate Japanese Americans to pursue his ambition.

Consider the following statement, giving Bendetsen full power and authority to him, as dictated by General DeWitt. Bendetsen claims it was given to the Commission on Wartime Relocation and Internment of Civilians, on July 9, 1981.

> "I hereby delegate to you all and in full my powers and authority under Executive Order 9066, which in turn has been delegated by the President to the Secretary of War, by the Secretary of War to the Chief of Staff, and by the Chief of Staff to the Commanding General of the Western Defense Command and Fourth Army. All rules and regulations of the Fourth Army, over which I have any control or authority, you have authority to suspend, as in your judgment may be necessary. You will take this action forthrightly, you will establish a separate headquarters, you will have full authority to call upon all federal civilian agencies, as provided in the Executive Order, and to call for assistance and cooperation of the State authorities as the President has in turn asked the Governors of the states concerned to provide. You will do this with a minimum of disruption of the logistics of military training, operations and preparedness, and with due regard for the protection, education, health and welfare of all of the Japanese persons concerned. You will, to the maximum, take measures to induce them to relocate voluntarily under your authority, in areas east of the Cascades, Sierra Nevadas, and north of the southern half of Arizona and New Mexico, so that the burden upon them will be at a minimum. You will make known that the Army has no wish to retain them at any time for more than temporary custody. It would be contrary to the philosophy and desires of the Army to do otherwise. These measures are for the protection of the nation in a cruel and bitter war, and for the protection of the Japanese people themselves.

You will use all measures to protect the personal property of Japanese, including crops."

(Statement was not dated, but most likely made on March 11, 1942.)

How much did Bendetsen's actions match the words of DeWitt? What we can assume is that all notices, exclusion orders, directives, etc., issued after March 11, 1942, with DeWitt's name on them, were in fact done by Bendetsen.

According to Weglyn (p. 69), Bendetsen was promoted from Major to Lieutenant Colonel on February 4, 1942, and ten days later to full Colonel, so that he could personally supervise the execution of EO 9066, which had not even been issued until February 19th. Strange, indeed.

In the book by deNevers (p. 128), Bendetsen states: "I was promoted to the grade of full Colonel with rank from February 1, 1942, which made me the youngest in that grade at that time." Even more curious is why Bendetsen was promoted, as he had not done anything of significance until after the "buck" had been handed down to him by DeWitt, on March 11, 1942.

Michi Weglyn (p. 69) described the Bendetsen plan for incarceration having involved three parts:

1. The issuance of an Executive Order, which would authorize the Secretary of War to "military areas," from which all persons who did not have permission to enter and remain to be excluded as a "military necessity."
2. The designation of military areas.
3. The immediate evacuation from these areas of all persons lacking licenses to reenter or remain.

Weglyn continues the discussion:

"The Army stratagem, which makes no mention of the Japanese for whom it was intended, was to become the basis of Executive Order 9066 issued by the President on February 19, 1942. It enabled the military, in absence of martial law, to immediately circumvent the constitutional safeguards of over 70,000 American citizens and to treat the Nisei like aliens."

In fact, the evacuation orders used the term "non-aliens" instead of the term "citizen," to hide the nefarious scheme to put us into the camps.

The term "military necessity" was used repeatedly to justify the removal of the people. It was not the first time it was used. Historians will remember that in 1831, the American government ordered four Native American tribes: Choctaw, Cherokee, Chickasaw and Creek, to abandon their ancestral lands in the Southeastern United States, to move "west of the Mississippi." The reason given for the removal was "military necessity." (See "Trail of Tears.")

Bendetsen claimed to have conceived, drafted and processed Executive Order 9066, authorizing creation of military areas to control and exclude civilians therein. He also stated that he conceived and organized the Civil Affairs Division and the Wartime Civil Administration of Western Defense Command, used to incarcerate us in the Assembly Centers. (Appendix B, p. 314, The Colonel and the Pacifist by DeNevers.)

Even the Final Report, attributed to General DeWitt, was authored by Bendetsen. We now know that military necessity was false. What else in that report was questionable? How much of the report influenced the decisions of the Supreme Court in the Korematsu, Yasui and Hirabayashi cases?

Given the above background, it seems clear that Colonel Bendetsen was an ambitious, manipulative, deceitful, self-serving individual who made a habit of promoting himself when it was in his interest, and protecting himself when it was not. Bendetsen was the person most responsible for the planned exclusion of Japanese Americans from the West Coast and incarceration in American concentration camps.

Questions about Bendetsen still linger. For example, why wasn't he promoted to General after doing such an efficient task of removing us from the West Coast? Why did he not only change his name to appear non-Jewish, but also change his nationality from Lithuanian to Danish? Did he know about Chiune Sugihara, who issued more than 2,000 visas to Jews in Lithuania, allowing them and their families to flee the Nazis through Russia, Chinaand Japan to safe havens abroad in 1939?

Bendetsen was never held accountable for his activities against the Japanese Americans. In 1950, he was nominated to be Assistant Secretary of the Army. At the confirmation hearings, the former Provost of the University of California, Monroe Deutsch, stated: "The appointment of a man whose utterances reveal him as possessing racialist points of view analogous to those of Hitler, would be most unfortunate." Despite the opposition to Bendetsen's nomination, he was confirmed.

Appendices

FOR MANY YEARS, those associated with Amache have wished for some type of formal relationship with the National Park System to preserve the camp site and its historic significance, so that what happened to Japanese Americans will never be repeated with another group of Americans. During the past ten years significant movement has been made toward fulfillment of that hopeful wish. Progress is being made, as the following documents reveal.

1. An apology from the California Grange, in March 2014, for their contributing role in the long and continuous pre-war hate activities against Japanese and Japanese Americans. The California Grange is a family fraternal organization. This very influential organization's activities were used to inflame and mislead the public of the target groups patriotism and loyalty to the U.S.
2. Granada Relocation Center (Amache) Comprehensive Interpretive and Conceptual Development Plan. A three day workshop was held in June 2006, at the National Park Service Intermountain Region service center to address a set of concerns detailed in the report.
3. In 2018, Senate Bill 2870 was introduced in Congress to provide for a three year study of Amache to determine the suitability and feasibility of the site as a unit of the National Park System. The bill was ultimately included as part of a Land Management bill signed by the President in 2019.

California State Grange

3830 U Street Sacramento, California 95817
(916) 454-5805 / fax: (916) 739-8189
president@californiagrange.org

March 25, 2014

David Lin, President
Japanese American Citizens League
1765 Sutter Street
San Francisco, CA 94115

Dear David:

On behalf of the members of the California State Grange, please accept this letter of apology to the Japanese American Community for a discriminatory period in our history, of which we are not proud.

The California State Grange started in 1873 and continues today as a fraternal organization supporting agriculture and communities. We have over 9,700 members serving 185 communities in the state.

Examining our past, we recognize that the Grange was a leader in organizing opposition to Japanese immigration, beginning in 1907. Along with the American Legion, the California State Federation of Labor, and the Native Sons of the Golden West, the Grange was active in the Asiatic Exclusion League.

The California Grange passed a resolution in 1907 which stated that aliens living in the United States should be barred from buying and owning land. The California Grange was instrumental in passage of the Alien Land Law of 1920, and the 1924 law ending Japanese immigration to the United States.

In 1922, the California Grange passed a resolution supporting federal legislation that resulted in the 1924 law that expressed "... the intense feeling of our people of the West in this matter, so absolutely vital to Christian civilization and the white races of our country."

These early seeds of racism sprouted after the bombing of Pearl Harbor, and the Grange supported the incarceration of Japanese Americans. In 1943, the Grange called for the deportation of all people of Japanese ancestry, aliens and American citizens alike.

In view of this history of discrimination, an apology is long overdue. The California State Grange, by unanimous vote of its member delegates recently passed a resolution calling for an apology to the Japanese American community. As President of the California State Grange, I present this letter of apology to the Japanese American Citizens League, with the request that it be shared with Japanese Americans across the country.

No words can compensate for the past injustice and loss of property, freedom and dignity, but I hope that this is a small step toward preventing a recurrence of racism and toward promoting equality for all people.

Sincerely,

Bob McFarland, President
California State Grange

Comprehensive Interpretive Plan and Conceptual Development Plan

Summary

At the request of The Friends of Amache and the Town of Granada, the National Park Service – Intermountain Region organized a three-day workshop to provide guidance and direction for interpretation and development at the Granada Relocation Center (Amache) National Historic Landmark. The meeting was held June 5-7, 2006. The purpose of this workshop was to improve the visitor experience at the site by exploring alternatives for site development and interpretation, while also incorporating long-term maintenance and preservation goals into the planning process.

A National Park Service (NPS) facilitator directed the workshop based on the following objectives:

- Define Amache's important stories.
- Explore how Amache's stories can be told to visitors.
- Where should Amache's stories be told?
- How should we maintain and preserve the Amache site?

Participants in the workshop included representatives from The Friends of Amache, the Town of Granada, Amache Preservation Society, Amache Club, National Trust for Historic Preservation, and the Intermountain Region of the National Park Service.

Site Background

On February 10, 2006, Secretary of the Interior Gale Norton designated Granada Relocation Center (Amache) a National Historic Landmark (NHL) for its national significance in illustrating the heritage of the United States. There are fewer than 2,500 such designations in the country.

The Granada Relocation Center, commonly known as Amache, is one of the ten Relocation Centers where Japanese Americans were incarcerated during World War II, following their forced removal by military authorities from the West Coast. President Franklin D. Roosevelt signed Executive Order 9066 on February 19, 1942. E.O. 9066 authorized the military to remove over 110,000 persons of Japanese ancestry – U.S. citizens and non-citizens – to the camps.

Between late August 1942 and mid-October 1945, over 10,000 people passed through Amache. At its peak, Amache housed 7,318 Japanese Americans, two-thirds of whom were U.S. citizens, in CCC-type barracks, surrounded by barbed wire and guard towers, manned by military police personnel.

Of all the Centers, Amache best conveys the regimentation, crowding, and lack of privacy that characterized the evacuation, confinement and relocation of Japanese Americans during World War II.

Statements of Significance

Significant statements reflect the National Historic Landmark's importance to the nation's natural and cultural heritage. The following statements describe the elements that distinguish Amache as a nationally significant site.

- Amache represents a time when American citizens of Japanese ancestry were denied their freedom and rights guaranteed by the United States Constitution.

- Amache has a rich documented history of the camp and the people that lived and worked there.
- Amache was the tenth largest city in Colorado at the time.
- The Amache site retains tangible historic resources, such as the foundations of camp facilities, remnants of koi ponds and gardens, the cemetery, and the same physical setting, isolated on the Colorado plains. All of these elements and resources combined can be used to tell stories, including the harsh conditions inmates endured while unjustly incarcerated, and their efforts to improve the physical environment during their time of confinement.
- Amache was the smallest of the ten internment camps.
- Amache was the only camp with concrete foundations and brick flooring in the inmate residential area.
- Amache's agricultural program was one of the largest of its kind.
- Ten percent of eligible inmates (men and women) volunteered for the United States military service. Over 30 were killed in Italy and France.

Primary Interpretive Themes and Subthemes

Workshop participants developed four primary interpretive themes and their associated subthemes. Primary interpretive themes are the key stories, ideas, and concepts of a National Historic Landmark. These themes lay the groundwork necessary to educate visitors about the site and to inspire visitors to appreciate and respect the significance of its history in our nation.

Primary Interpretive Theme A:

- Fueled by fear, war hysteria, avarice, and panic, the U.S. government failed to protect the constitutional rights of its citizens following the attack by Japan at Pearl Harbor on December 7, 1941, by ordering and implementing the forced removal and incarceration of more than

112,000 Americans of Japanese ancestry into "American concentration camps." Over 7,500 were moved into Amache in August/September 1942, after they had been removed earlier and put into "assembly centers" like Merced County fairgrounds and Santa Anita racetrack.

Subthemes:

- The entry of the United States into World War II resulted in the creation of Amache and the other nine camps.
- The Japanese American eviction, confinement, and relocation experience raises the question of the role and violation of Civil Rights in American society.
- Will similar actions happen in the future?
- Discuss the historic use of the term "concentration camp" and its present usage.

Primary Interpretive Theme B:

- From chaos to community: Japanese Americans incarcerated at Amache attempted to develop a sense of community similar to those from which they had been evicted. They struggled to maintain their family structure and strove to retain a sense of normalcy in Amache.

Subthemes:

- Discuss the role and impact of location.
- Discuss the role and impact of physical structures.
- Discuss the role of the camp's operation and logistics.
- Discuss the role of communications (e.g., newspapers, etc.).

Primary Interpretive Theme C:

Relationships among individuals, groups, and the communities connected to Amache continue to evolve; these relationships have encompassed the spectrum from hostile to amicable.

Subthemes:

- The creation of Amache resulted in some injustices to Granada residents leading to long term distrust between parties (e.g., local residents, the federal government, War Relocation Authority, Japanese American community, and inmates of the camp).
- Inmates and Coloradans experienced a range of interactions from the reinforcement of prejudices to forging new relationships.
- Evolving partnerships and cooperation.

Primary Interpretive Theme D:

Even after the camp closed, the struggle to overcome injustices continues to linger, resulting in great impacts on individuals and traditions.

Subthemes:

- Changes are still occurring as democracy within the United States continues to evolve: this directly and indirectly impacts individuals and traditions in both a positive and negative way.
- The need to be vigilant to protect constitutional rights of Muslims and Arabs following 9/11 and in light of the "War on Terror."
- Immigrant groups adapting, acculturating or assimilating to American life impacts on families, traditions, culture and generations.

The workshop participants listed a lengthy and detailed set

of suggestions on how to implement the themes and subthemes which will not be included here.

Since the meeting in 2006, many of the suggestions have been met but others are still being discussed on strategies and actions to be taken.

Five examples of site improvements at Amache during the past 12 years:
1. Reconstruction of the original Amache water tower.
2. Construction of a replica of one of the Amache guard towers.
3. Movement of an original recreation building to its original site.
4. Development and maintenance of a museum in Granada by the Amache Preservation Society, under the direction and guidance of teacher/principal John Hopper and his students.
5. Acquisition of two buildings to expand the museum. One to serve as a research facility and the other to serve as a visitors' center.

115TH CONGRESS
2D SESSION
S. 2870

To authorize the Secretary of the Interior to conduct a special resource study of the site known as "Amache" in the State of Colorado.

IN THE SENATE OF THE UNITED STATES

MAY 16, 2018

Mr. GARDNER (for himself and Mr. BENNET) introduced the following bill; which was read twice and referred to the Committee on Energy and Natural Resources

A BILL

To authorize the Secretary of the Interior to conduct a special resource study of the site known as "Amache" in the State of Colorado.

Be it enacted by the Senate and House of Representatives of the United States of America in Congress assembled,

SECTION 1. SHORT TITLE.

This Act may be cited as the "Amache Study Act".

SEC. 2. DEFINITIONS.

In this Act:

(1) SECRETARY.—The term "Secretary" means the Secretary of the Interior.

(2) STUDY AREA.—The term "study area" means the site known as "Amache", "Camp Amache", and "Granada Relocation Center" in Granada, Colorado, which was 1 of the 10 relocation centers where Japanese Americans were incarcerated during World War II.

SEC. 3. AMACHE SPECIAL RESOURCE STUDY.

(a) IN GENERAL.—The Secretary shall conduct a special resource study of the study area.

(b) CONTENTS.—In conducting the study under subsection (a), the Secretary shall—

(1) evaluate the national significance of the study area;

(2) determine the suitability and feasibility of designating the study area as a unit of the National Park System;

(3) consider other alternatives for preservation, protection, and interpretation of the study area by the Federal Government, State or local government entities, or private and nonprofit organizations;

(4) consult with interested Federal agencies, State or local governmental entities, private and nonprofit organizations, or any other interested individuals; and

        (5) identify cost estimates for any Federal acquisition, development, interpretation, operation, and maintenance associated with the alternatives described in paragraphs (2) and (3).

(c) APPLICABLE LAW.—The study required under subsection (a) shall be conducted in accordance with section 100507 of title 54, United States Code.

(d) REPORT.—Not later than 3 years after the date on which funds are first made available to carry out the study under subsection (a), the Secretary shall submit to the Committee on Natural Resources of the House of Representatives and the Committee on Energy and Natural Resources of the Senate a report that describes—

    (1) the results of the study; and

    (2) any conclusions and recommendations of the Secretary.

In 2019 a bill was introduced, passed and signed by the President to study the feasibility of the Amache site becoming a part of the National Park System. If successful, Amache can join two other major tourist attractions in the southeast section of Colorado: Bent's Fort, honoring the pioneers who developed the area, and secondly a site remembering the massacre of American Indians at Sand Creek on November 29, 1864.

Almost 40 years ago I remember when a redress bill was introduced in Congress to study what happened to Japanese Americans during WWII that led to their evacuation and incarceration into "assembly centers" and "relocation camps." A congressional committee was formed, a set of nationwide meetings held, and redress passed. Hopefully it will not take as many years for Amache to become a unit of the NPS such as Alcatraz, the State of Liberty, Sand Creek, etc.

1933 – The San Francisco island of Alcatraz became a maximum-security federal prison. Today, the island is an historic site operated by the National Park Service.

Presentation for the Romero Theatre Group (2012)

SEVENTY YEARS AGO SOMETHING HAPPENED; extraordinary and unprecedented.

What happened? Who, what, where, why, and how?

This is an American story.

The Fifth Amendment to the Constitution states that no American shall be deprived of life or liberty without due process of law. No American.

We were American citizens, born in the USA. We had done no wrong. There were no charges made against us. No trial. No justice.

We lost our homes, our businesses, our livelihood, and most of all – our freedom.

Our world was turned upside down.

Pledging allegiance to the flag of the United States of America was an exercise in hypocrisy and futility.

We were removed from our homes, our community, our state and place in concentration camps. Why?

When the evacuation orders were posted in our towns and sent to our homes, the words were as follows:

> "All persons of Japanese ancestry, both aliens and non-aliens, will be evacuated from the above designated area by 12:00 o'clock noon, etc., etc."

Why did they call us citizens "non-aliens" and if we were non-aliens, all in this room who think they are citizens are also non-aliens. Indeed, a strange set of words to use.

What was meant by the words, "all persons of Japanese ancestry?" Is ancestry a crime?

What about persons of mixed ancestry – some of whom were infants and toddlers, abandoned and placed in orphanages? Father Hugh Lavery of the Catholic Maryknoll Center in Los Angeles posed the question to Colonel Karl Bendetsen about some of the children in his center who were half Japanese or even quarter Japanese.

The Colonel replied: "I am determined that if they have one drop of Japanese blood in them, they must go to camp." Why did Bendetsen say those words? Who was Bendetsen? (Architect, advocate and administrator of the evacuation and incarceration. Check him out on the internet.)

The children were sent to Manzanar. No exceptions.

What about veterans of Japanese ancestry who had served in the U.S. Army in World War I? No exception. (One killed himself to avoid evacuation.)

What about Ernest Kuramatsu, who was half French, born in Canada, who served in the Canadian Army in WWI and was studying to be an artist in Carmel, California? He was part Japanese, so he was sent to Merced Assembly Center and then to Amache. No exception.

Once we were in the camps, why did men (and some women) volunteer to enlist in the Army to fight the enemy Germans, Italians and Japanese in Europe and the Pacific Islands?

Why did others resist the draft orders? What happened to them?

Hundreds of books and thousands of articles have been written about this shameful period in American history – and yet, why is it that millions of Americans have little or no knowledge of what happened to their fellow Americans? Why?

The Patriot Act, passed by Congress following 9/11, allows

our government to detain Americans and others for an indefinite period without due process – no charges, no trial.

Sound familiar? Who will be the victims next time? Arab Americans? Mexican Americans? Chinese Americans? Mormons? Muslims? Catholics? Jews? Sikhs?

Some final comments: We were victims of racism, fear and hysteria, economic greed, lack of political integrity in our leaders, Machiavellian manipulation by military and political leaders, and misinformation in our newspapers, on our radio, and in films.

And finally: We should remember that when our national leaders preach to the rest of the world about the need to observe human rights and practice democratic principles, we do so carefully, given our own history of successes and failures in these areas.

Robert Fuchigami, 2012

About the Author

Robert Y. Fuchigami, Ed.D.
University of Illinois, 1964.
Institute for Research on Exceptional Children.

BORN IN 1930 AT MARYSVILLE, CALIFORNIA. In May 1942, his family of ten: father, mother and eight children, were evicted from their 20 acre fruit and vegetable farm in Yuba City, California, by the U.S. Army and sent by train to Merced (California) Detention Center (assembly center). In September 1942 they were moved again by train to the Amache Concentration Camp (Granada Relocation Center). They were incarcerated behind barbed wire fences for three years, during which time they lost their farm – home, truck, equipment, etc.

With nothing to return to in California, the family moved to Greeley, Colorado, when released from Amache in September 1945. Robert completed high school, enrolled in college an completed two years before joining the U.S. Navy, when the Korean War began in 1950. After four years, he resumed his college education and completed a B.A. and M.A. at San Jose State University. He taught in elementary and secondary schools in San Jose and Hayward, California, before receiving a federal grant in 1960 to pursue a doctorate at the University of Illinois, Institute for Research on Exceptional Children. He was awarded the degree in 1964.

Work Experience: He taught summer session at Sacramento

State University in 1962. He was a State Consultant with the Illinois State Department of Education (1963). He began a teacher training program in Special Education at the University of Hawaii in 1964. He left Hawaii in 1966 to serve as the Field Coordinator of the Northwest Regional Instructional Materials Center, based at the University of Oregon. In 1968, he moved to Sonoma State University in California to start a teacher training program in Special Education. During the summer, he taught special education at the University of Wyoming (1971 and 1973), and at the University of Wisconsin, Whitewater (1972). He served as the Chairman of the Education Department and later Dean of Graduate Studies at Sonoma State University. He took one year leave of absence to work for the National Council of Exceptional Children in Reston, Virginia (1977), and as State Director of Special Education for California (1985). He retired in 1992.

Bibliography

Bosworth, Allan R. *America's Concentration Camps.* W. W. Norton. 1967.

Burton, Jeffrey F., Mary M. Farrell, Florence B. Lord and Richard W. Lord. *Confinement and Ethnicity: An Overview of WWII Japanese American Relocation Sites.* National Park Service. Department of the Interior. 1999.

Chang, Gordon H. Morning Glory, *Evening Shadow: Yamato Ichihashi and his internment writings, 1942-1945.* Stanford University Press. 1997. Includes excerpts of a diary kept by Stanford Professor Ichihashi during his evacuation and incarceration in Amache.

Daniels, Roger. *Concentration Camps USA.* Hold, Rhinehart, Winston. 1972.

Daniels, Roger. *The Decision to Relocate the Japanese Americans.* J.B. Lippencott Co. 1975.

Daniels, Roger, Sandra Taylor and Harry Kitano. *Japanese Americans from Relocation to Redress.* University of Utah Press. 1986. (Excellent resource.)

deNevers, Klancy Clark. *The Colonel and the Pacifist: Karl Bendetsen and Percy Saito and the Incarceration of Japanese Americans during World War II.* Salt Lake City: University of Utah Press, 2004. (A must read for anyone interested in knowing the person who was the architect, advocate and first administrator of camps to incarcerate Japanese Americans.)

Dressman, Denny and John Elliff. *Beyond the Camps.* Vis-Op

Publishing. Sterling, Colorado 2018. (Through interviews and stories of 17 successful Japanese Americans like Min Yasui, Bill Hosokawa, and others in Colorado, the authors provide a positive view of former inmates of the exclusion incarceration period.)

Fisher, Ann Reeploeg. *Exile of a Race*. Sidney, British Columbia: Peninsula Printing Co., Ltd. 1965. (Little publicized book, but one of the better accounts of the entire exclusion and incarceration period.)

Girdner, Andre and Anne Loftis. *The Great Betrayal*. MacMillan Co. 1969.

Gordon, Linda and Gary Okihiro. *Impounded*. W. W. Norton Company. 2006.

Grodzins, Morton. Americans Betrayed: Po*litics and the Japanese Evacuation*. Chicago: University of Chicago Press, 1949. (Scholarly analysis by a distinguished Professor of Political Science.)

Gruenwald, Mary Matsuda. *Looking Like the Enemy*. New Sage Press. 2005.

Harrington, Joseph. *Yankee Samurai*. Pettigrew Enterprises. 1979.

Hartz, Erica. *Last Witnesses*. Palgrave/MacMillan Press. 2001.

Havey, Lily Yuriko Nakai. *Gasa Gasa Girl Goes to Camp*. University of Utah Press. 2004. (This remarkable book is a true tale of an adolescent growing up in Amache. The author utilizes a combination of photos, prose and paintings to relate her years in the camp.)

Harvey, Robert. Amache. *The Story of Japanese Internment in Colorado during WWII*. Taylor Trade Publishing. 2004. (Well researched book. Includes excerpts of interviews with former inmates of the camp.)

Holsinger, M. Paul. Amache: *The Story of Japanese Relocation in Colorado*. Masters Thesis, University of Denver. 1960.

Hosokawa, Bill. *Nisei*. William Morrow Publishing Co. 1969.

Inada, Lawson. *Only What We Could Carry*. Heyday Books. 2000. (Excellent resource.)

Johnson, Melvyn. *At Home in Amache: A Japanese American Relocation Camp in Colorado*. Colorado Heritage. 1989.

Kitano, Harry H. L. *Japanese Americans: The Evolution of a Subculture*. Prentice Hall Inc. 1968.

Lillquist, Karl. *Imprisonment in the Desert. The Geography of World War II Era in the Western States*. Central Western University. September 2007 (Chapter 3 is on Amache. Excellent coverage of the Amache site: geography, history, people, etc.)

Matsumoto, Valerie J. *Farming the Home Place*. Cornell University Press. 1993. (Chapter 3, on Merced Assembly Center and Chapter 4, on Amache, are excellent. Rich in detail.)

McNaughton, James C. *Nisei Linguists*. Department of the Army. 2007.

Nakano, Mei. *Japanese American Women*. Mina Press. 1990.

Newton, Jim. *Justice for All*. Riverbend Books. 2006.

Nishimoto, Richard S. *Inside an American Concentration Camp*. Tucson, Arizona: University of Arizona Press. 1995. (The focus is on the Poston Arizona Concentration Camp. Includes information about the All Center Conference at Salt Lake City.)

Niya, Brian (ed.). *Japanese American History: A to Z*. Reference from 1868 to the Present. Japanese American National Museum. 1993. (Excellent resource. Niya is now with DENSHO and has written an Encyclopedia of Japanese Americans.)

Okubo, Mine. *Citizen 13660*. New York: Columbia University Press. 1946. (This book contains pen and ink drawings that accurately depicts the evacuation and incarceration experience.)

Robinson, Greg. *By Order of the President*. Harvard University Press. 2001.

Robinson, Thelma. *Nisei Cadet Nurse*. Black Swan Mill Press. 2005.

Reeves, Richard. *Infamy*. New York: Henry Holt and Company. 2015. (Award winning journalist of books like *President Kennedy: Profile of Power*, this informative book is written in a style both interesting and scholarly. Highly recommended.)

Schrager, Adam. *The Principled Politician*. Fulcrum Publishing. 2008.

Sone, Monica. *Nisei Daughter*. Little Brown Publishing. 1953.

Spicer, Edward H., Ansel T. Hansen, Katherine Luomala and Marvin K. Opler. *Impounded People: Japanese Americans in the Relocation Centers*. Tucson, Arizona: University of Arizona Press. 1969. (An inside look at life in the camps by four social scientists who worked as WRA Community Analysts. Includes an excellent bibliography.)

Sterner, Gordon. *Go For Broke*. American Legacy Historical Press. 2008.

Tateishi, John (ed.). *And Justice for All. An Oral History of the Japanese American Detention Camps*. New York: Random House. 1984. (Information from taped interviews with camp survivors.)

tenBroek, Jacobus, Edward N. Barnhart, and Floyd W. Matson. *Prejudice, War and the Constitution*. Berkeley, California. University of California Press. 1954 and 1968. (Scholarly volume written by three members of the Faculty of Law at the University of California in Berkeley.)

U.S. Commission on Wartime Relocation and Internment of U.S. Citizens. *Personal Justice Denied*. Washington: Government Printing Office. 1982. (Report of the Congressional Commission assigned to investigate the evacuation and incarceration of Japanese Americans and Aleutian Islanders during WWII. A "must read.")

Weglyn, Michi. *Years of Infamy*: The Untold Story of America's Concentration Camps. New York: William Morrow Co. 1976. (Considered a "classic" by many for the extensive research conducted by a former inmate. The author uncovered governmental information about the exclusion, incarceration and resettlement experience. Excellent resource.)

Wei, William. *The Strangest City in Colorado: The Amache Concentration Camp*. Colorado Heritage, Winter 2005. Pages 2-17.

Williams, Joyce E. and Alice M. Coleman. *Lest We Forget. The Japanese and America's Wartime Mistake*. Cummings and Hathaway. 1992. (Excellent book that covers the exclusion/

incarceration period using the theme of internal colonialism to explain what happened. Very good chapter on Amache. This unusual book includes about 60 pages of poems by Alice Coleman, who lived in Tamai Towers in Denver. The facility housed a large group of Japanese Americans, whose stories about Amache and other camps served as a basis for the poems. Overall, a must read which has been overlooked by many.)

Fiction – Include references to Amache

Creel, Ann Howard. *The Magic of Ordinary Days*. Viking Penguin Press. 2001.

Dallas, Sandra. *Tallgrass*. St. Martins Press. 2007.

Means, Florence Crannell. The Moved Outers. New York: Walker and Company. 1945. (This Newbery Honor Roll book was written by the author after she had spent some time in Amache with Catherine Ludy, a teacher in the camp. Excellent book for children.)

Okada, John. *No-No Boy*. University of Washington Press. 1979.

Rizzuto, Rahna R. *Why She Left Us*. Harper Collins Publishers. 1999.

Booklets, Pamphlets and Newspaper Articles

Kusaba, Henry (ed.). *Amache Colorado*. Documentation Section. Reports Office. April 5, 1943.

As Time Goes By 1942-1998. Reunion booklet. Las Vegas. October, 1998.

Internment of Japanese Americans. Documents from the National Archives. Kendall Hunt Publishing Co. (n.d.)

Douglas, Truman B. *70,000 American Refugees: Made in U.S.A.* Pamphlet of the Citizens Committee for Resettlement of the Congregational Christian Church. (n.d.)

Fuchigami, Robert Y. *Amache: An American Concentration Camp in Colorado*. 1999. (Booklet was part of a grant awarded to the author by the California Civil Liberties Public Education Act of 1998. The other part was a binder of photographs of Amache.)

Fuchigami, Robert Y. *Granada War Relocation Center – Amache Colorado*. "*Return to Amache.*" Amache reunion, June 19-21, 1998. Colorado Springs and Amache campsite.

Fuchigami, Robert Y., Flora Lee Ganzler, Mei Nakano and George Nichols. *Curriculum Guide* for the Sonoma County Schools Office of Education. 1991.

Granada Pioneer. Mimeographed newspaper distributed three times a week in Amache, 1942-1945.

Nakashima, Tyler. *Amache Onichee Prowers: Amache, The Granada Relocation Center*. Davis, California. 1994.

Onlooker. Amache High Yearbooks. 1943, 1944, 1945.

Pulse. Amache Literary Magazine. Volume 1, No. 1 (n.d.)

Mixed Media: DVDs, TV and Radio Interviews

Calling Tokyo. Japanese American radio broadcasters, like Sam Masami Ono, whose families were incarcerated in Amache, released to Denver to assist the U.S. and British armed forces in the Pacific region. This DVD was produced by Gary Ono in 2013.

Camp Amache: The Story of an American Tragedy. A DVD (also in VHS) by Don Dexter. Available from Dexter at: (719)275-8475, or email: dondexter@comcast.net. 2006. Color.

DENSHO Interview with Bob Fuchigami 5-14-2008. One of several interviews conducted with former Amacheans by DENSHO. Available on DVD.

Enduring Communities. A DVD highlighting events from the Diversity, Civil Liberties, and Social Justice National Conference in Denver, Colorado, July 3-6, 2008, by the Japanese American National Museum. One segment is on the field trip to Amache.

Leap of Faith. How a Buddhist Temple in the small rural town of Sebastopol, California, was saved from burning by a young group of Christian youth during WWII. Only 18 minutes of this DVD was broadcast on KRCB-PBS station.